A GUIDE TO THE PERFORMING ARTS OF

BALINESE DANCE, DRAMA & MUSIC

by I WAYAN DIBIA *and* RUCINA BALLINGER

illustrations by BARBARA ANELLO

TUTTLE Publishing

Tokyo | Rutland, Vermont | Singapore

Published by Tuttle Publishing, an imprint of Periplus Editions (HK) Ltd.

www.tuttlepublishing. com

Text © 2004 Rucina Ballinger and Dr. I Wayan Dibia
Illustrations © 2004 Barbara Anello

ISBN 978-0-8048-4183-2

Distributed by
North America, Latin America &Europe
Tuttle Publishing, 364 Innovation Drive,
North Clarendon, VT 05759-9436, USA.
Tel: 1 (802) 773-8930; Fax: 1 (802) 773-6993
info@tuttlepublishing.com
www.tuttlepublishing.com

Japan
Tuttle Publishing, Yaekari Building, 3rd Floor,
5-4-12 Osaki, Shinagawa-ku; Tokyo 141 0032.
Tel: (81) 3 5437-0171; Fax: (81) 3 5437-0755
sales@tuttle.co.jp
www.tuttle.co.jp

Asia Pacific
Berkeley Books Pte Ltd, 61 Tai Seng Avenue, #02-12,
Singapore 534167.
Tel: (65) 6280 1330; Fax: (65) 6280 6290
inquiries@periplus.com.sg
www.periplus.com

Indonesia
PT Java Books Indonesia, Kawasan Industri Pulogadung,
JI. Rawa Gelam IV No. 9, Jakarta 13930.
Tel: (62) 21 4682-1088; Fax: (62) 21 461-0206
cs@javabooks.co.id

13 12 11   6 5 4 3 2 1

Printed in Singapore

TUTTLE PUBLISHING® is a registered trademark of Tuttle Publishing, a division of Periplus Editions (HK) Ltd.

Pages 2–3: *Jegog* bamboo ensemble. **Page 4:** Rangda being chased in the Barong dance. **Page 6:** Cokorda Rai as the Condong in Legong Keraton. **Page 7:** Taruna Jaya dancer in three poses at Puri Saren, Ubud.

Contents

Preface

The performing arts of Bali are rich, vast and complex. Virtually every form of music, dance, drama and shadow puppet play has its origin as a function for a ritual, if not a ritual in itself. Even the more contemporary art forms have strong links to the past. Balinese dance and theater are spectacular—from lavish costumes to rhythmic darting eye movements to incredible improvisation of the performers. Balinese gamelan music is electrifying and soothing at the same time. Balinese shadow puppetry is shrouded in mystery and echoes ancestral voices. The pursuit of artistic knowledge begins at a very early age in Bali and is supported by the entire community. Basic cultural values are passed on via the arts and reflected in the stories told and the movements executed.

This book is meant to be a guide to the three main types of performing arts in Bali: traditional dance and drama, gamelan (an ensemble of from two to fifty instruments) and shadow puppetry. We want the visitor to be able to recognize a particular art form and understand it better, albeit briefly. This is not meant to be a comprehensive guide to Balinese performing arts, but rather one that will lead the reader to appreciate the more common forms that will be seen while in Bali. Illustrations of many of the genres will assist in the visualization of the forms. Selected reading and discography lists are at the end of the book.

We begin by contextualizing the forms as to their function and how they are learned. Then we focus on each specific form, beginning with gamelan music, then shadow puppetry, and finally dance and theater forms. Gamelan and dance/theater are, in fact, not separated in the field, but we have separated them for the purposes of this book. The performing arts in Bali developed at a phenomenal rate during the twentieth century. This book focuses on the history and development of traditional performing arts and how these have influenced contemporary gamelan music, dance, theater and puppetry.

We hope this book will enhance your enjoyment of the performing arts of Bali. Take it along with you to local performances.

Selamat menonton!
Enjoy the show!

The Performing Arts in Bali

Dance, drama and music are much more than mere performances. They are spectacles of color and sound, but their main purpose is to please the deities and ancestral spirits. Art, if not a ritual in itself, is a part of the ritual. The arts express the values that the Balinese hold dear, such as balance and harmony. *Taksu*, or spiritual charisma, is the pinnacle of energy which every Balinese performer strives for to mesmerize both the human and divine audience.

Bringing the body down from the tower to place in the sarcophagus, at a royal cremation in Gianyar, 1992.

Dance of Topeng Tua, an old man, one of the introductory characters in the Topeng dance-drama.

Almost every ritual has some type of art form associated with it. A temple festival has gamelan music and probably a shadow puppet play and a mask dance. A wedding might have a Joged (flirtatious social dance), and cremations have marching gamelans accompanying the procession to the cemetery. The Balinese love anything that is *ramai* (festive, full and colorful), and the more the better. It is not surprising to have at least two different types of music happening at the same time at a temple festival.

Part of the reason why there is so much artistic activity on this tiny island is that the soil, rich in volcanic minerals, produces an incredible array of agricultural produce. This easy availability of food allows more leisure time in which to make art. Yet the old adage that every Balinese is an artist is simply not true. What is true is that children (particularly boys) are encouraged to create. Any village that can afford it, will have its own gamelan orchestra as well as music and dance clubs.

Balinese Religion

Balinese religion is a blend of ancestral worship, animism, Hinduism and Buddhism. The traditional village (*desa adat*) is the center of the universe for a Balinese, and the concept of mutual cooperation echoes in the interlocking rhythms of the gamelan. Every village has at least three communal temples and their festivals are occasions for music, dance, theater and puppetry to honor deities and ancestors. Certain traditional rituals must be conducted in temples to ensure health and prosperity for the villagers. Particular deities enjoy seeing plays about themselves during the temple festival. Some villages are known for a specific form. When someone dies, the family may go to a trance medium to find out what the deceased would like to have done during the cremation. Classical performing arts will be sustained in Bali as long as their ritual aspects continue to have meaning.

Balinese performing arts are not static. Many changes in musical and dance styles have occurred over the years and changes are taking place due to the influx of wide-ranging influences from outside Bali. It is important to note that while most Balinese prefer the classical forms, they also welcome new, innovative art forms.

An Expression of Cultural Values

There is no word for art in Balinese; *seni* (art) is an Indonesian word. The Balinese refer to an "artist" as a skilled person (*tukang*) rather than an artist. The word for dancer or actor is *pragina*, which means "someone who beautifies." Since art is such an integral part of all ritual, it cannot be easily taken out of context (although tourism certainly has changed this concept!). Traditionally, performers do not receive payment when playing for a temple festival or ritual; they do it for devotional reasons.

One of the basic philosophies in Bali is *rwa bhineda* ("two differences"). Like the Chinese theory of yin–yang, this is the principle of balance in the world:

male/female, day/night, good/evil, right/left. It is expressed in the performing arts in many ways: "good" puppets are on the puppeteer's right while "bad" ones are on his left. Dance movements are executed on both sides, and musical instruments are tuned so that two tones from two different instruments create a harmonic. Balance is of utmost importance to the Balinese. In dance, the basic position is a mastery over imbalance. In the puppet world, the ideal character has balance in personality.

Character types in performance are divided into *alus* (refined) and *keras/kasar* (strong/coarse) with male and female characters within these two, a reflection of this system of duality. Traditionally, a dancer performed one type which conformed most to her or his body type: a tall and slender dancer would be more suited for a prince or princess while a short and robust dancer would play a servant or warrior. Today, dancers tend to be well rounded and can play multiple roles; specialization is now fading.

Performance Venues

The traditional *kalangan* (performance space) can be a simple clearing in front of someone's home, a field in the village or a large permanent structure, open on three sides with an elevated stage. The audience sits on the floor or on chairs. The *kalangan* could be in the outer courtyard of a temple, with a *langse* (split curtain) at one end. This is flanked on two sides by the gamelan players and the audience sitting wherever they can see. Generally, there are no tickets, reserved seats or timetable. The performance begins when the performers have all gathered, been fed and are made

up. In the village, most shows do not usually begin until around nine at night and they last for several hours. Some dance-dramas go on until the wee hours of the morning while *tari lepas* (non-dramatic dances) may last only a few hours.

Protocol

Visitors are welcome to watch performances at temples, family rituals and official events as long as they are dressed properly and do not disrupt any of the proceedings. In a ritual setting, this means wearing full *pakaian adat* (temple clothes). This is extremely important as the Balinese have stringent rules about

Villagers bringing Barong and Rangda masks to Pura Saraswati, a royal clan temple in Ubud, to receive offerings from the people.

In the Barong dance, performed here at Batubulan, clowns are allowed the freedom to express themselves through make-up and facial expressions.

The Temple Compound

Within a temple compound are three courtyards. The *jeroan* (innermost courtyard) is where the majority of shrines are located and images of the deities are housed, and where people come to pray and bring their offerings to be blessed. The *jaba tengah* (outer middle courtyard) houses the gamelan pavilion, temple kitchen and a few shrines. The *jaba* (outer courtyard) is outside the temple with a large hall for performances and where the gambling and food stalls are located. The Balinese reduce their actions in the outer courtyard, lessen their words in the middle courtyard, and once in the innermost sanctum they quiet their thoughts. The temple is activated in ritual every 210 days (or in some cases every 12 lunar months—called an *odalan*) by being decorated with flags, gilded cloths and offerings. These rituals are rooted in Agama Hindu Bali or the Balinese Hindu religion, which is an integral part of the everyday life of the Balinese.

jeroan (innermost courtyard)

jaba tengah (outer middle courtyard)

jaba (outer courtyard)

A dancer at Ubud Kaja prepares for his role as the heroic bird Jatayu in the masked form of Wayang Wong, which depicts the great epic of the *Ramayana*.

dress. If the performance is at a public gathering, then modest and neat clothing is the norm. Photography is usually allowed, except for some of the most sacred forms. In most cases, flash and video are permissible, but using flash while worshippers are praying is frowned upon. If there is a particular performance you want to see in a traditional venue, such as a temple festival, get there early and prepare to wait (enjoy some *kopi Bali* at a local *warung* or food stall and get to know the locals). These venues are usually outdoors so bring along something inconspicuous to sit on, such as a small mat.

Division of Three

The Balinese believe that things can be divided into three parts: *utama* or the highest part (head), *madya* or middle part, and *nista* or lowest part (feet). When at a performance, particularly in a ritual setting, it is best to not be seated higher than someone else. Standing on a temple wall or steps to get a better view is considered very rude, but most Balinese will be too polite to tell you. Please do not walk or stand in front of people praying. Remember that these performances are often rituals and not an entertainment.

Sacred and Profane

Since the advent of mass tourism in the 1970s, there has been a lot of discussion about what constitutes sacred dance. The Barong-Rangda dance, which is performed daily in Batubulan, for example, is actually a re-enactment of an ancient ritual pared down to 60 minutes. Yet the masks used for tourist shows are not the same ones used for rituals. Context establishes the degree of sacredness, but the Balinese prefer not to see their most sacred dance and music forms put up on a stage. This is something that scholars and artists are still trying to agree on.

In 1971, a seminar was held by LISTIBIYA (the Balinese Arts Council) on Sacred and Profane Dances. The general consensus was that the degree of sacredness depended on where the performance was held. A tripartite division emerged: *wali* ("offering") refers to the most sacred forms, which often but not always occur in the *jeroan* (innermost courtyard of a temple). These forms are the ritual or offering themselves, as in the case of Wayang Lemah ("daytime" shadow puppetry, performed without a screen and without much of a human audience), Topeng Pajegan, Rejang, Baris Gede, Mendet and Sanghyang. The second category is *bebali*. These are forms done in conjunction with a ritual or ceremony but are not necessarily the ritual themselves, such as Gambuh, Wayang Wong and Wayang Kulit. The third category is *balih-balihan* meaning "that which is watched" and has no direct religious or ritual importance. All *tari lepas* (non-dramatic dance) as well as Joged Bumbung, Janger and others fall into this secular category.

Yet the lines are blurry; the exorcistic Calon-arang drama, for example, which often results in the performers and/or audience falling into trance, is done in the outermost courtyard yet could be glossed as *wali*. For the Balinese, the most important aspect is to have the utmost respect for the forms meant for their deities and that no defilement takes place. But when Sanghyang trances done for tourists have fake trance, it gives pause for thought.

Taksu

In Bali, there is no specific deity of dance or music or puppetry. Performers pray to their ancestors before leaving home to ensure success. They also pray at the temple where they are performing for *taksu* to descend into their souls. *Taksu* is an energy, a type of spiritual charisma that exceptional artists (and healers) are blessed with. It has little to do with technical precision, as there are performers who are perfect in their execution but lack that extra something, while there are those less skilled but who are able to bind their audience to them. *Taksu* can be passed down from a parent to a child or from a teacher to a pupil. A performer can have *taksu* at one performance and the following night fall flat. A mask can possess *taksu* and assist the actor in making it come alive. An entire gamelan orchestra can possess *taksu* regardless of who plays in it.

Having *taksu* is possessing the ability to hold your audience, to become magnetic and enchanting (in the full sense of the word) on stage. In the West, some might call this stage presence, but it is much more than that as there is a definite connection with divine forces. A performer prays for *taksu* to please the mortal audience and the divine one as well.

Another concept which assists in the attainment of *taksu* is the tripartite idea of *bayu* (energy), *sabda* (inner voice) and *idep* (thought). In order for *taksu* to appear, these three elements must be in balance.

A dancer (or puppeteer) must have energy in order to move, his or her inner voice or convictions must be present in order to perform well, and there must be clarity in the thought process.

Even though the number of performers has increased greatly over the last century, those with *taksu* have decreased. Modernization and globalization are partly responsible for this. The attention span is shorter and concentration is less strong than it was in the past. Musicians, dancers and puppeteers have reasons other than solely devotion (money and fame among them) for performing at a temple ceremony. Just a generation ago, children in a village would get so excited about performing at the next temple festival with their uncles and fathers and brothers accompanying them on the gamelan and all their neighbors and relatives watching. Today there are after-school activities, video games and, of course, television. All of this has an impact on the arts, yet there never seems to be a shortage of dancers and musicians.

Blessing of the Barong and Rangda. Sacred masks are given offerings of food and flowers, placed on the ground, to appease the spirits of chaos.

Moving between Two Worlds: Belief and Magic

The seen (*sekala*) and the unseen (*niskala*) worlds are equally important to the Balinese, and they move from one to another with ease. A dancer moves from the world of the ancestors to the world of the audience. A puppeteer brings the ancestors down to the screen in the shape of shadows. In daily life, in life cycle rituals and in performance, the Balinese are ever aware of the spirits and energy surrounding them and the importance of establishing "balance."

The princess in Arja performs a simple yet symbolic gesture, that of opening the curtain–stepping from the secular world into the realm of the sacred.

The Balinese religion is Hinduism, yet the texture is much richer and more ancient than the Indian Hinduism which came to Bali from the ninth century. One of the most important aspects of the belief system is ancestor worship. When people die, they are cremated and purified in elaborate rituals and worshipped as ancestral deities. These ancestral spirits, if remembered and appeased, help their descendants. If neglected and forgotten, they may wreak havoc upon the family.

Moving between the two worlds of *sekala* (seen, conscious) and *niskala* (unseen, subconscious) is something the Balinese do with ease on a daily basis. This can be manifested in actions as familiar as beeping the car horn when crossing a bridge to alert the *tonya* (river spirits) who live there, asking their permission to pass, or praying to a deceased family member for a successful performance.

Influence on Performing Arts
The influence of the *niskala* world plays a large part in the performing arts. Puppets in the shadow play are actually thought of as deities or ancestors, and masks have a spirit of their own and must be propitiated. Gamelan instruments as well as dance costumes all have their own special cleansing rituals every 210 days: *tumpek krulut* for gamelan, *tumpek landep* for *keris* (daggers), and *tumpek wayang* for puppets and dance paraphernalia.

Certain objects can be imbued with supernatural power, such as a *keris*, mask or gamelan instrument. In many *sanghyang* traditions, brooms, jar lids, dolls and rattan wands become infused with the spirit. This can be seen in its essence in performances of magic: Calonarang, Basur and various types of dances and dramas which use the mask of Rangda the witch. The performance itself is a way to balance energy which has become shaky. The world is tipping too

much towards chaos and needs uprighting. Often this occurs during the sixth lunar month (November–December) when disease is more prevalent at the beginning of the rainy season (see pp. 56–7, Rejang). Many villages have specific rituals to ward off *pengiwa* (black magic). Practitioners of left-handed magic create havoc and hurt others by casting spells over people that cause illness.

Right: Young dancers pray before images of ancestral deities in the temple to ask their blessings for the forthcoming performance.

Trance

The Balinese accept trance as an ordinary occurrence, a way of communicating with the gods, spirits and ancestors. Certain masks, types of music and performances, such as Calonarang, are better able to induce a trance state than others. In Sanghyang (pp. 58–9), for example, a trance state is induced by a number of elements: first, there are sacred songs sung to invite the spirit of divine entities into the bodies of the dancers; secondly, the heavy smoke from the frankincense helps to induce a hypnotic state and, thirdly, group expectation: the villagers hope that the Sanghyang will go into trance. This is a type of group hypnosis and the reason that trance usually occurs in controlled, sacred spaces. One never goes into trance without others around to witness and validate it. Trance may occur in performance as well as in religious rituals. It is a sign that the deities have truly descended.

Legong dancers at Pura Desa Sumerta go into a trance after performing for 20–30 minutes. The power of the headdresses is said to induce altered states of consciousness.

A performer so completely transforms him- or herself into the character being played that an altered state is achieved. This makes the performer more susceptible to magical spells being sent their way by a member of the audience. There are special prayers and mantra that performers recite before going on stage and amulets they wear for protection. In some plays, such as Calonarang, the Rangda dancer or the *dalang* (puppeteer) calls on all the *leyak* (witches) of the village to come to the stage area to test their magical powers. This type of "magical dueling" was quite common in the past. Many older Balinese can tell you of the time a Calonarang puppeteer performed in their village, and the next morning either a local witch or the puppeteer was dead, depending who won.

A less dangerous way for a performer to move between two worlds is in the performance itself. As soon as the dancer moves through the liminal space of the *langse* (curtain), he or she goes from the present to the past—a time that lives on in the performance. Some dancers linger a while at the curtain, teasing the audience, singing or speaking from behind, hesitating to emerge. Others come directly out, either miming the opening of the curtain or moving right into the dance. Whichever way it is done, the dancer becomes not necessarily a specific personage but the essence of the character. His or her own ego is forgotten. Many performers can tell of the exhilaration of doing a role well, of pleasing not only the human audience but the divine as well.

Actors, dancers and puppeteers perform for a number of religious events. The Balinese classify their rituals (*yadnya*, literally "sacrifice") into five main types: *dewa yadnya* for the deities, such as temple festivals; *bhuta yadnya* for the nature spirits who create chaos; *manusa yadnya*, rites of passage such as a tooth-filing ceremony or a wedding; *pitra yadnya*, death rites; and *rsi yadnya*, purification rites for a priest. Some dances are only performed at specific times, such as Baris Poleng for cremations or Rejang at a temple festival; others could be done as entertainment during any of the rites.

Masks used in the sacred Topeng performance are blessed before being worn. Shown here are the Penasar, Dalem and Sidhakarya masks.

Learning to Perform

Everyone learns by watching and copying. Here, in Bali, it takes a more active form, especially on the teacher's part. In dance, a teacher molds the pupil's body to her own so that every nuance of the style can be absorbed by the student. In music, the teacher sits on the opposite side of the instrument and plays it backwards while teaching! The whole learning process is a community event. Rehearsals take place in the *bale banjar* or community hall for all to observe.

Said to be the incarnation of the late Ketut Madra of Sukawati, I Made Gede Panji Prameswara, Madra's grandson, manipulates the shadow puppets of the Wayang Kulit with ease.

Manipulation of the limbs is one of the keys to absorbing the style of the teacher. Left to right: I Ketut Maria (Mario), one of Bali's best known choreographers and dancers in the 1920s, teaching Kebyar Duduk. The suppleness of his limbs extends to that of his pupil; I Nyoman Kakul teaching his young grandson Ketut Wirtawan the Baris dance, 1974. I Made Jimat teaching a young girl in the 1990s.

A Part of Daily Life

The integration of the arts into Balinese daily life is one of the great beauties of this culture. Children begin learning at an early age. They hear the gamelan music while still in the womb, and as babies, held in a family member's lap, they are encouraged to dance with their hands before they can walk. The arts are not something locked away in a studio to be brought out for public viewing only when finished. On the contrary, rehearsals are held at the *bale banjar* for all to see, comment on and criticize. Women set up small food stalls and sell their goods to the audience and passersby. Mistakes provoke laughter, yet this is all part of the learning process. Young dancers cannot be embarrassed by a crowd's watchful eyes. If they make an error, they will be corrected in public during a rehearsal, and receive critical comments from family members, neighbors and onlookers. This toughens them for performance.

Children begin formal study at around seven years old, although some might start earlier. They find themselves performing before an audience even before they have perfected their musical or dancing abilities. This is intentional and teaches them humility. Moreover, the purpose of the performance is not perfection but an offering to their ancestral deities and gods and goddesses. The intention and feeling with which it is performed is most important. School recitals and other performances in the community give students a chance "to show their stuff" and gain confidence.

A child born into an artistic family begins to learn at home by simple observation and imitation, then by more formal lessons with one of the family members. Children go along to performances with relatives to help them dress, make up and prepare for the show. In this way, they learn not only about movement, but about the whole context of dance, theater and music. A village can be famous for a particular art form, such as Gambuh, Arja or Legong, and the teachers there are sought out by other performers.

Sekaa or Clubs

In many villages, there are numerous gamelan or music and dance clubs (*sekaa*). These groups usually consist of about fifty members who all voluntarily support the activities of the gamelan club. There are many types of *sekaa* but the groups described here are specifically for gamelan or music and dance. Within the *sekaa* are musicians, dancers, managers, costumers and drivers. They are paid for their services; most of the money goes into a communal kitty, and the rest is divided up among the members. There is fierce pride within the *sekaa* as well as friendly competition among rival groups. A performer also may perform independently of the *sekaa*. Dancers and actors who belong to different *sekaa* may be asked to perform together on occasion for dance-dramas such as Arja, Topeng and Drama Gong. This one-time ensemble is called a *bon* group. Therefore, a sponsor can hand-pick the group of actors and dancers.

There are social organizations that promote artistic endeavors. The *banjar* or local hamlet often owns a gamelan orchestra that can be played at any time, a fact that children may take advantage of. If they have a *sekaa*, weekly rehearsals are set and all members are obliged to attend. There are usually performances at local village functions, such as at temple festivals, where the *sekaa* will show off its latest pieces.

Aside from the traditional *sekaa*, there are now *sanggar* or dance and music studios. These first started to sprout up in the city of Denpasar due to the demand at the time for dance lessons. The onset of tourism provided further opportunities for performing and teachers became in great demand. There are usually one or two well-known teachers in the *sanggar* and dancers study specific dances in order of difficulty. At the end of each level, a certificate is awarded along with a public performance. If you can get to one of these "graduation" ceremonies, it is great fun as the entire family usually shows up to cheer on their progeny. The students perform in full costume and make-up, oftentimes with a full gamelan orchestra, sometimes to a cassette tape.

Physical Learning

The Balinese way of teaching is unique. A beginning dance student stands behind the teacher and mimics the movements. The teacher sings the melody of the

A Typical Dance Class

Traditionally, dance is learned without mirrors. The child first mimics the form of the teacher. Once she has memorized the basic movement patterns, her teacher then moves behind and manipulates her limbs, at times making total body contact. In this way, the body feels what it is supposed to do and how it should place itself without needing to look in a mirror. Teachers today are much less strict than thirty years ago when the rule was to pound (sometimes literally with a stick!) the dance into the pupil. If that happened today, there would be few students in dance classes.

Above left: Ni Ketut Arini Alit teaching at home. Without mirrors to guide them, the students must move exactly as the teacher does.

Above right: Ni Ketut Arini Alit manipulates the arms of her pupil, at the same time kicking her feet into the correct position.

Left: "Men" Sena of Tista teaching Legong. Fine adjustments for arm placements let the student know how to move properly.

gamelan, gives drum and gong cues as well as calls out the names of steps and basic instructions. "Get that elbow up!" "Bring your body closer to the ground." Once the basic choreography is learned, the teacher moves behind to mold the student's body. This enables the student to feel exactly where the wrist and elbow should be placed and how the back is aligned. Traditionally, mirrors were not used so the student had to rely on this kinesthetic transference of energy

Ni Ketut Arini Alit teaching dance on the television program "Bina Tari" in 1980. Beginning in the late l970s, "how to learn dance" shows began cropping up on local TV stations. This has had an impact on the standardization of dance throughout the island.

Sanghyang dancers being blessed before performing to ensure that trance will occur. Dancers who perform for religious rituals will, at the very least, be blessed with holy water at the performance site. Alternatively, they will pray at the local temple.

to know how to move. The teacher kicks the students' feet up and jerks their heads from one side to another. It is a very physical way of learning.

The method of teaching music is quite similar. At first, teacher and student sit facing one another, each with his or her own instrument. The teacher plays "backwards" while the student mirrors the hand motions. At times the teacher kneels behind the student and actually moves the hands to the correct position on the instrument. It is possible to know who a performer studied with simply by their style, as traditionally a student learns from only one teacher. There are particular teachers so well-known for the "results" that they draw out of their students that people come from great distances to study with them. Prior to Indonesia's independence in l945, it was common for teachers to travel to another village and live for months at a time to teach the locals there music, dance, singing or puppetry.

Formal Learning

Since the 1960s, it has been possible for the more serious student to specialize in one of three fields—dance, music or shadow puppetry—at SMKI (Sekolah Menengah Karawitan Indonesia or High School of Performing Arts) or at ISI (Institut Seni Indonesia or Indonesian Arts Institute). SMKI was formed in 1960

with the purpose of producing teachers who would return to their villages and help develop the performing arts. ISI began in 1967 as ASTI (Akademi Seni Tari Indonesia or the Indonesian Dance Academy) and is still often called that although its status changed to the College of Indonesian Arts (Sekolah Tinggi Seni Indonesia or STSI) in 1988 and to ISI in 2003.

The original goal of SMKI (then KOKAR) was to create teachers as well as to preserve traditional forms and develop new ones. Graduates brought back to their village what they had learned, and local versions were neglected and eventually forgotten. Students at both schools are extremely well trained in a variety of art forms with a myriad of teachers so they no longer follow one teacher's style, but have the "school" style.

During the Soeharto era (1966–98), ASTI/STSI/ISI became known as the Super-Sekaa because it was called upon by the central government in Jakarta to produce extravaganzas with hundreds of performers. Since the economic crisis of l998, those performances have faded into memory. Some of the most innovative performance comes out of STSI today. Composers are given free rein to create and are encouraged to collaborate with other musicians and performance artists from all over the world (see pp. 102–3).

Visitors are welcome on the campuses. Classes are held Monday to Saturday from 8 a.m. to 1 p.m. See Resource Guide for details (see p. 105).

The Role of Television in Learning

The latest "teacher" is television. Once a week, a show called "Bina Tari" (Preserving Dance) is aired on the local TVRI station in Denpasar. Started by Ni Ketut Arini Alit in 1979, it demonstrated basic steps and some of the more popular dances so people in remote villages could learn them as well. Today it is carried on by the popular teacher I Nyoman Suarsa. As not everyone has a gamelan in their *banjar*, cassettes have become a popular way to learn. "How to learn" cassettes repeat the same song over and over again, making it easy to practice the dances. Needless to say, this has assisted in the standardization process.

Rituals for Dancers

Traditionally, a serious student of dance has a number of rituals to observe. The first is the *mesakapan* where the student becomes "married" to the mask or headdress (*gelungan*) of the particular dance form being studied. Often this ritual is performed for a gamelan club to marry musicians to instruments so they will feel just like a family and their playing will be compact and harmonious.

Melaspas is a ritual to purify a new object and transform the original material into a new entity. For example, a headdress made of leather now becomes a performer's crown. The wood of a mask is reborn as a personage. The object's status changes from ordinary to sacred. Often a dancer takes those objects to a priest to be blessed in a ceremony called *pasupati*, in which they are infused with magical power. From that time onward, the object must not touch the impure ground and must be handled with reverence.

Mewinten is a ritual to purify a person rather than an object. The person gains a higher status. There are various levels of *mewinten*. Those who want to learn the sacred songs and stories in the traditional palm leaf manuscripts (*lontar*) must go through a *mewinten*. *Dalang* or puppeteers are purified in a number of *mewinten*, as they are considered to be priests once they have completed their training. This ritual enables the performer to become one with the object (headdress, mask, puppet or instrument). The three levels are *mewinten alit* (simple purification) with flowers; *mewinten madya* (middle purification), usually performed inside a temple, and the final stage is *mewinten agung* (large purification) that consists of staying three to four days in a temple and being blessed with copious amounts of holy water and offerings. This is usually reserved for priests, but Topeng Pajegan (solo mask) dancers are encouraged to complete all three.

Preparing for a Performance

Serious performers recite a number of prayers before they perform. According to I Ketut Kodi, a well-known *dalang* and Topeng actor, before performing he first prays at home in his family temple where he asks for *taksu* (spiritual energy) for his performance to be a success. At the performance site, he prays to the deity residing in the local temple and receives holy water. Before going on stage or beginning his puppet show, he asks the inhabitants of the space for their permission for the performance. The many spirits lurking about which can cause mischief must be

placated. Then he blesses the objects he will use (masks and puppets) with simple offerings, invoking their spirit. At the conclusion of the show, he conducts another small ceremony to send the spirits back home.

Before the first notes of a concert are struck, the gamelan must be blessed, usually by the local priest or someone in the gamelan group itself. The spirit of the large gong is invoked so that good sounds will be produced. All of the musicians are blessed with holy water. The instruments are believed to have souls and must not be stepped over.

A *dalang* also performs numerous rituals on the day of a performance. On leaving the house, mantras or prayers are said. Before entering the stage area, he notices out of which nostril his breath is strongest: if the right, Brahma will perform, if the left, Wisnu, and if equal, Iswara or Siwa will do the honors. Once behind the screen, offerings are made, the space is sprinkled with holy water and the gods are asked to descend to witness the performance.

For those performers involved in more magically dangerous roles, such as Rangda, along with the men and women who may try to stab her (see pp. 70–5), there are certain prohibitions they must abide by for 24 hours prior to the ritual. These include not eating certain foods, abstaining from sexual relations and avoiding a corpse.

Left: Probably no more than three or four years old, this young male Kebyar dancer, at his first recital, has already mastered the basic stance and moves.

Right: Final exam for Kebyar Duduk at the Warini dance studio, Art Centre, Denpasar. Part of learning dance is performing in front of your peers and family in a very public space. These events are open to the public and often televised on one of the two local Balinese television stations. Aside from the pride of being on stage, there is always the chance of snagging a trophy for being in the top three!

Dance Movements

"But what does it all mean?" This is a common lament heard among visitors when watching Balinese dance for the first or fiftieth time. With so many hand gestures, eye movements and stances, it is difficult to decipher the meaning. Balinese hand gestures are not storytelling movements as in East Indian dance; rather, they embellish expressions of the body. All movements are done on both the right and left sides to establish harmony and cohesion.

Elegant in positioning, Balinese hand gestures are used to emphasize emotional expression.

Most Balinese dance movements are abstract, even in those dances which tell a story. The movements have little to do with the progression of the plot. The Balinese love seeing how well a performer executes and interprets a dance. It is similar to watching a performance of the *Nutcracker*; it is not so much the story as the skill of the dancers that is compelling. What is important is that special quality of a performer which can transport the audience to a different sphere, something known as *taksu* (spiritual charisma) (see p. 11).

Agem

The *pokok* (foundation) of the dance is an asymmetrical basic stance or *agem*. In right *agem*, the body weight is on the right foot with the left foot in a modified third position or 45 degrees in front of the right foot. The torso is shifted to the right with the shoulder blades squeezed together—giving the back that typically arched look of female Balinese dance roles. For most female dances and refined male roles, the arms are bent at 90 degree angles with the wrists lower than the elbows and the hands bent back at the wrist. The right hand is level with the eyes; the left hand is level with the breast and the head is tilted slightly to the right. The left *agem* is the opposite. For a strong male style, everything is bigger: the forearms cut through more space and the shoulders are lifted close to the ears. In the female *agem*, the feet are one fist length apart; the refined male *agem* has the feet two fist lengths apart and the strong male *agem* is very wide.

The posture is a reminder of the importance of balance in Balinese culture. Since the *agem* is unbalanced, it is difficult to hold, with the weight usually centered on one or another foot, not both. It thus demonstrates human control over imbalance, even if transitory. An *agem* is where all dances begin and end and all movements progress from it, but the position is held only momentarily.

Transitions from one static posture to another (*tangkis*) come in a variety of moves. A locomotive as opposed to a stationary transition is called *tandang*. A common one in Kebyar style is called *angsel*: the feet and arms do quick, energetic bursts of movement from one side to the other, reflected in the music.

Seledet, Keeping Your Eyes on the Eyes

Throughout Indonesia, only Balinese dance utilizes eye movements. Many people believe that its origin is East Indian although there is no concrete evidence of this. In an eight-count phrase, the eyes dart to the side on count six or seven and return to the center on eight, marked by the strike of a gong.

Learning How to Walk

Dance students spend hours just learning how to walk. The walking pattern for women (*ngumbang*) is a sensual swaying of the hips stemming from the knees. The body traces a figure eight (*luk penyalin*) or an S pattern (*ombak segara*, literally "ocean waves") on the floor. The lower the dancer can get to the ground (*ngaad*), the better. For males, learning how to "walk" can take weeks, if not months. This is the *pokok*, where one's strength originates from. In the basic male walk (*malpal*), the legs are turned out in a diamond-shaped pattern with one heel lifted towards the opposite knee. The chest and shoulders are lifted up and the torso remains still. It is imperative to be as low as possible. The Balinese live close to nature, so this striving to become one with the earth is evident in the dance. Contrast this to ballet where the dancers defy gravity with every move.

Breath is the vital force of the dance and is reflected in the movements. The up and down movement of the *agem*, called *meangkihan*, symbolizes breath itself. Dancers are trained to control their breath, hold it and expel it consciously in order to give maximum power to the movement.

Facial and body expressions (*tangkep*) are also crucial, although today's dancers tend to neglect this part of their training. The mouth should be in a semi-smile with the eyes alive and vibrant. To denote anger, the shape of the mouth changes to a more neutral expression and the eyes widen (*nelik*). The body also expresses emotion and must be full of *bayu* (energy). A dancer whose performance is lackluster will be called *cara anak won* ("like someone worn out").

Movements from Nature

Very few hand gestures have symbolic meaning. Only a few movements actually depict specific things: *ulap-ulap* (peeping), *nuding* (sending a message or being angry) and *manganjali* (both hands in a prayer position in front of the chest in a gesture of welcome). Many movements are abstractions of things in nature, such as *ngelo* (ripe rice stalks blown by the wind), *kijang rebut muring* (deer swatting flies from its face), *lasan megat yeh* (lizard skittering above water), and *capung manjus* (dragonfly bathing). There are abstractions with little reference to content or plot. Many of the movements are named after their function: adjusting the flowers in the headdress (*nabdab gelungan*), lifting up the dance cape (*nyingsing*), and touching the bracelet (*nabdab gelang kana*). In fact, performers are constantly adjusting their costumes while on stage.

No Balinese dance is complete without the quick, fluttering vibrato of the fingers. Princess's fingers may quiver elegantly, a warrior's with pulsating energy. This is symbolic of the *bayu* radiating from the dancer's center. It weaves its way up and out into the fingers. In a master dancer, this happens naturally; in student dancers, it must be taught.

The fan is an essential part of both Legong and Kebyar style dances. It is made out of a number of small bamboo sticks covered with gold-painted cloth. Each side of the fan is a different color, adding to the beauty of the movements. There are various names for how the fan is held. Musical punctuation can be exaggerated with the fan. The fan can be static, twirled, held at the chest or closed and pointed at someone in anger or in threat.

There are many variations in the eye movements of dancers: to the side (*seledet leser*); to the upper corners (*seledet tegeh*); to the ground and back to the center (*nyegut*, describing the center vein of a leaf); with the neck and head tilted to the side and returned to the center with the eyes squinting, then widening, symbolizing a tiger awakening from a nap (*ngeliyer*); and when the dancer catches the eye of a member of the audience, looks away shyly and then focuses again on that person (*seledet nganceng*).

Ni Komang Suharriati depicting the many moods of youth in the Taruna Jaya dance. This dance is one of the more difficult in the repertoire due to the rapid changes from strong to soft movement, as well as fleeting changes in mood reflected in bodily and facial expression.

Make-Up and Costuming

A large component of stage performance is costuming and make-up. The Balinese take this quite seriously and would never consider performing on stage without elaborate alterations in their presentation. Hours can be spent on transforming into princesses, demons and animals. Each dance and every character have their particular type of dress and headdress which clues the audience into knowing who is what. Pots of various colors, hair extensions, false mustaches, razor blades, hair pins and the very necessary safety pins are all part of the dancer's cache.

Backstage, a female dancer portraying a *sisya* or student of the witch applies her make-up using low lighting and a small mirror. The effects are as dazzling as if she had a professional dressing room at her disposal. Hundreds of fresh frangipani flowers, with one big red hibiscus in the center, are the crowning touch to her make-up.

Right: Backstage at Pura Dalem Tebesaya, Peliatan. Most dancers can dress themselves, and they can do it in a flash. Sometimes, however, a professional "dresser" will be called upon, especially to tighten the torso cloths so that a smoother line can be achieved.

Putting on a New Face

A basic make-up formula is used for both males and females as well as make-up for specific character types and roles. Since the Balinese use their eyes so much in dance, make-up for the eyes is the most important. The eyes are widened by thick black lines on top and bottom, with a fishtail at the sides. In the past, soot from wood-burning stoves was used for this purpose. The eyebrows are arched and colored. Traditionally, the entire face may have been shaved to emphasize the largeness of the eyes. Since the advent of televised performances, blue and orange eye shadow are used, whereas none was applied in the past. Foundation, rouge and lipstick are used by both male and female actors. The latest touch is glitter gel on the arms!

Probably the most interesting part of stage make-up is the *cundang* (dot between the eyebrows) symbolizing the Third Eye of strength and concentration. This is usually a simple red or white dot, sometimes an upside-down black V, and one or three white dots (*urna*) at the outer corners of the eyebrow. Some dancers recite a mantra while drawing this and ask for divine inspiration (*taksu*). Some say these three dots symbolize the Hindu Trinity of Brahma, Wisnu and Siwa. Others claim it is pure decoration. Today, performers use toothpaste for these dots, whereas in the past *pamor* (powdered limestone) was used.

In dance-dramas, the make-up is more elaborate. Many attributes of Wayang Kulit puppets are transferred to costumes for actors, particularly for the headdresses. Servant and clown characters and demons sport the most dramatic make-up. The entire face may be painted red, such as that of Rawana in the Hindu epic *Ramayana*. White dots are painted in semicircular lines around the face for clowns, demons and antagonistic kings. Princes sport huge mustaches and bushy eyebrows. Demonic females have fangs painted on. Monkeys have furry eyebrows and a jutting jaw piece.

Good Hair Days

For female offering dances, the hair is twirled leaving the end dangling in back. In most other dances, the hair is tucked up inside the *gelungan* (headdress). Women playing male roles tuck their hair up and under in a page-boy. As demons and witches, female

performers let their hair flow loosely. Men often wear wigs or hair extensions for strong characters. Refined roles sport headdresses partially covering the dancer's head. Flowers are tucked behind the ears.

The Body as Something To Be Wrapped

Both males and females wrap themselves in many layers of costumes to restrict movement as well as to have a beautiful, sleek line. For refined female roles, a 2.25– or 2.5–meter *kain* (fabric) is wrapped around the hips to the ankles. The front flap falls center. This cloth has silk-screened designs in *prada* (gold leaf).

Princesses and maidservants, such as the Condong in Arja and the female dancer in Oleg Tambulilingan, may wear an additional piece of material at the bottom of the *kain* as a train. Tucked between the dancer's feet, she flips the fabric out of her way as she steps. In refined male roles, the *kain*, pleated and draped on the left hip, is wrapped from hip to knee, freeing the legs to move easily. Women and refined male dancers often wear white, long-sleeved shirts.

For strong male roles, white trousers are worn with *setewel* (beaded leggings). A 2–3 meter-long white cloth is draped around the chest with a *kancut* (long pleated "tail") hanging in front. A gold-patterned *saput* (cape) of *prada* worn from the chest to the knees and left open in the center is covered by a short velvet coat with long sleeves. The *badong* (beaded circular collar) and *keris* (dagger) tucked into a belt above and behind the shoulder blades complete the costume.

For all female and refined male roles, a plain 8-meter-long *sabuk* (sash) is wrapped as tightly as the dancer can stand, then covered in an equally long gold-leafed *sabuk*. Various leather or cloth accessories, such as belts, arm- and wristbands, collars and *lamak* or *awiran* (hanging cloth panels), are held in place by elastic bands and safety pins.

Crowning Glory

Headdresses and masks are the holiest parts of the costume. Because the head itself is considered holy, the headgear is often consecrated by a priest and kept in the village or family temple, or in the highest place in a dancer's home. The headdress demarcates the character of the dance, drama and puppets, indicating if the character is *alus* or *keras*. Headdresses are given offerings on auspicious days and before being used in a performance. Incense is stuck in the headdresses as part of the blessing. Even dancers performing at tourist venues pray for a successful performance and bless their headdresses and masks.

In dance-dramas, the headdresses often have pandanus leaves sticking out above the ears and *girang* ("happy") leaves hanging down in front. Both of these plants have mystical protective powers. The *girang* leaves are are said to help the dancer be calm and confident during the performance.

Most headdresses are topped with flowers, some with only a few red hibiscus or white frangipani, others with a field of flowers. Refined royal male figures and female roles such as Legong have *bancangan* ("wire trees") filled with tiers of frangipani flowers to symbolize a mountain, the seat of the gods, which quiver at every head movement. Balinese pray with flowers, and dance is indeed a type of prayer.

Left: Ida Bagus Nyoman Mas as the demon Rawana. Demons often sport red faces, exaggerated eyebrows and mustaches and have the requisite fangs.

Middle: Ni Komang Suharriati in Taruna Jaya make-up and headdress. The typical make-up for *tari lepas* (non-dramatic dances) comprises accentuated eye make-up with a layer of blue on the lids and red and gold just under the brows. The thick line of white on the bridge of the nose is to make it appear more aquiline. A headcloth folded in the *dara kepek* ("slain pigeon") style is particular to this dance.

Right: I Nyoman Budiartha, a strong male dancer of the ancient Gambuh dance, wears modern style make-up. All facial hair is exaggerated and his eyes sport the now traditional blue, red or gold eyeshadow.

What is Gamelan?

Gamelan is the set of instruments which make up an ensemble. This could be as few as two *gender* (metallophones) or as many as sixty different percussive instruments. The way the instruments are played and tuned, and the cacophony of sound produced—clashing cymbals, booming gongs and clanging keys, all with a complex drum beat holding it together—give gamelan its unique flavor. There are over thirty different types of gamelan ensembles in Bali.

The History of Gamelan

The first written evidence of gamelan is found in the *Sukawana* and *Bebetin prasasti* (metal inscriptions) from the ninth century. The terms *parapadaha* (drummers) and *pamukul* (percussionists) from the *Sukawana prasasti*, and *pabunjing* (*angklung* player) and *pabangsi* (*rebab* player) from the *Bebetin* manuscript indicate gamelan activities existed during the Bali Kuno (ancient Bali) period.

According to a noted musician, the late I Nyoman Rembang, gamelan can be divided into three categories. Ensembles in the *tua* category (old or ancient, prior to the fifteenth century) are seven-tone *pelog*, which are found mostly in Bali Aga villages of North and East Bali. These do not use drums and the melodies are eerily haunting. *Madya* ensembles (middle or sixteenth to nineteenth century) developed in the courts with drums and knobbed gongs. The *baru* (modern or twentieth century to the present) feature drumming and complex interlocking parts.

Most gamelan originally came from the courts of Java. During the Majapahit kingdom (some call it the Golden Age of Hindu–Buddhist civilization), from 1343 to 1511, art flourished under the patronage of the royal families. Bali was a vassal state of Majapahit at this time. When Islam took hold in Java, many members of royalty and their courtiers moved to Bali, bringing with them their belief system and their arts.

The Dutch, who had colonized Java since the 1700s, had only limited control in parts of North and West Bali from 1849 until the turn of the century. In 1906, they invaded South and East Bali, eventually gaining control over the entire island. With both administrative and military power in their hands, the influence of the palaces declined, along with their patronage of the arts. Another phenomenon occurred during this time: the birth of the Gamelan Gong Kebyar. Villagers in North Bali, where this started, melted down the keys on their old gamelan to transform them into new Kebyar orchestras (see p. 25).

The late I Made Lebah, a famous drummer from Peliatan, plays the drum for the Gamelan Pelegongan. The drum is the dynamic leader in a Balinese ensemble.

The *grantang*, a bamboo xylophone of the Joged Bumbung ensemble, is played using a pair of sticks with round rubber tips. The left hand plays the melody, while the right hand provides the elaboration.

Metallophones

A metallophone is an instrument where metal is struck to produce a sound. There are two kinds of metallophones in gamelan: *gangsa*, which are hit with one mallet, and *gender*, which are struck with two mallets. The keys are suspended over bamboo resonators cased in beautifully carved jackfruit or teak wood. Some of the *gangsa*, such as the *gender rambat* below, have carvings from traditional Balinese stories or fables worked on them. Each note hit must be immediately damped using the left hand, otherwise the sound becomes "muddy." *Gangsa* players pride themselves on their "clean and crisp" playing, especially when playing the *kotekan* or interlocking beats.

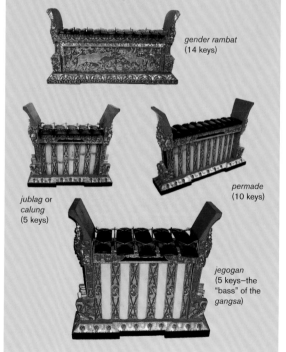

gender rambat
(14 keys)

jublag or
calung
(5 keys)

permade
(10 keys)

jegogan
(5 keys—the
"bass" of the
gangsa)

22

"Bursting open" and "sudden burst of flame" are only two ways to translate the word *kebyar*, which most definitely describes the music. Until 1915, gamelan music was rather monotone in its melodic and rhythmic configurations. Drastic changes in the instruments occurred in North Bali during this time. The incredible energy of Gamelan Gong Kebyar sounded discordant to some Balinese back then. Yet this was a reflection of the social situation; the destabilization of society could be heard in this new music. Up until this time, the music created a mood, an ambience; it filled the space with gentle notes and embraced the listener. Kebyar, on the other hand, pervaded the space in an aggressive way.

Composer and choreographer I Gede Manik of Jagaraga village in Buleleng is thought to be one of the precursors of this style. By the mid-1920s, Gong Kebyar had spread to the south of Bali, and by the 1930s it was well established throughout the island.

The instruments are all percussive with two exceptions: the *suling* (end-blown bamboo flutes) and the *rebab* (two-stringed bowed lute). The majority are metallophones (*gangsa* and *gender*) with 7–14 metal keys hung over bamboo resonators, spanning 2–3 octaves, and struck with a *panggul* (mallet).

Musical Principles

A number of musical principles are important within the gamelan. The musicians must play as one ensemble, to be *nges* (musically tight). There is no room for individuality, so hours and hours of rehearsal can go into preparing for a performance.

All of the metallophones are tuned in pairs to the same pitch but one instrument is tuned slightly higher than the other, resulting in a phenomenon known as "beating" when the two notes are struck simultaneously. This results in a beautiful shimmering sound (*ombak* or "wave") which permeates the entire ensemble, referred to as *ngumbang ngisep* ("bee sucking honey"); the higher note is called *pengisep* and the lower one *pengumbang*.

Paired tuning extends to gongs and drums, classified as male or female. The lower pitched drum (*kendang wadon*) is female and the higher pitched one (*kendang lanang*) is male. The female drum cues musicians and dancers alike. The large hanging gongs are also identified as male and female.

The most striking feature of Balinese music is the use of interlocking configurations (*kotekan*). This involves two *gangsa*, two *reyong* or two drums, each pair playing complementary parts which consist of *polos* ("simple"), the downbeat, and *sangsih* ("differing"), the upbeat. For the cymbals in the marching Balaganjur ensemble and Kecak (vocal chanting), a third part is added. Each part on its own sounds incomplete, but once partnered, produces a rich and full texture of sound.

Playing the instruments requires quick reflexes. A key is struck with the mallet held in the right hand, and as soon as the next one is struck the fingers of the left hand damp the previously struck key to stop its sound. *Gender* damping is done with the sides of the wrists and requires great dexterity and coordination (see p. 51). When playing complicated *kotekan*, it is imperative that each note be struck and damped clearly so that the sound does not become "muddy."

Gongs and Colotomic Structure

Balinese music is generally performed in an eight-beat phrase called a gong cycle, with the gong marking the end on beat eight. This is the opposite of Western music where the emphasis is on the first beat. Other gongs divide the phrase into smaller units. This is called colotomic structure. The gong cycle is symbolic of the never-ending cycle of life. The Balinese conceptualize time as a loop. This is evident in their cyclical calendar. The belief in reincarnation of the soul also mirrors the idea of cycles.

The most prolific instrument in the gamelan is the *gangsa* or metallophone. Struck with a hammer with one hand and damped with the other, an extraordinary sound is produced.

This inverted kettle gong (*reyong*) set is played by two pairs of players, one pair playing the *polos* part and the other pair playing the *sangsih*. Aside from the drum, this is the most difficult instrument to master in the gamelan.

In the colotomic structure of a *tabuh* (musical piece), the pace is kept by the *kempli* or *kajar*, a small flat gong on a short stand or held in a musician's lap and struck with a wooden beater. The large gong (*gong agung*) is struck on beat eight, the *kemong* on beat four, and the *kempli* on beats two and six, for example. The *kempur* is a medium-sized gong and alternates with the large gong, punctuating phrases. The small *klenang* is struck on the offbeat.

The *ugal* plays the main melodic line while the other *gangsa* play *kotekan* to elaborate the melody. The *jublag* play the core melody while the bass-like *jegogan* strike every two or four notes. The *reyong* and *ceng-ceng* play off one another and fill in around the *gangsa*. The *suling* and *rebab* elaborate the melody. The drums set the rhythm and tempo. In general, there is no virtuoso playing, although a group may be known for its superb drummers or complex *kotekan*. An entire group can be called *bergaya* ("flashy").

No music notation is used; everything is learned entirely by rote. When learning a new piece, the teacher calls out the notes. Occasionally, a composer may write down the core melody but none of the *kotekan* is noted. Gamelan groups fiercely guard their trademark compositions, yet it is easy for others to figure out the tune simply by listening to a cassette recording and copying it.

Tuning within the Ensemble

A Balinese gamelan is not tuned to one common scale, but to itself. A village can request a particular tuning for its gamelan when having a new one made or an old one refurbished. Musicians are familiar with both scales—*pelog* and *slendro*—which roughly compare to major and minor scales in Western music. The scales are not absolute, for *pelog* and *slendro* refer to intervals between notes as opposed to actual pitches. *Pelog* can be a four-, five- or seven-note scale of uneven intervals. *Slendro* can be a four- or five-note scale with roughly equal intervals.

The Balinese use the solfa names (*ding, dong, deng, dung* and *dang*) with a gap after *deng* and *dang* for the more common *pelog* scale. An example is E-F-G-B-C. *Pelog* and *Slendro* can be further broken down into two *saih* (scales). *Saih pitu* (seven-note) is found in the Gambuh, Gambang, Semaradhana and Semar Pagulingan ensembles. The more common *saih lima* (five-note) is used in Gong Gede, Gong Kebyar, Gamelan Pelegongan and Gamelan Bebarongan. Gamelan Jegog of West Bali is the only ensemble with a four-note *pelog* scale.

A typical *slendro* scale could be construed as A-C-D-E-G. This approximates the Western pentatonic scale and is used in Gender Wayang, Joged Bumbung, Gamelan Wayang Wong and Gamelan Parwa. The four-note *slendro* scale is used by Gamelan Angklung, although a five-tone Gamelan Angklung in North Bali is common.

Battle of the Bands

During the 1950s, a new phenomena called *mebarung* occurred where two different gamelan groups would perform against one another on stage. Oftentimes they did the same pieces so that the audience could judge which was the better or more innovative group. Today, *mebarung* refers more to a friendly evening of music from two well-matched groups.

Kebyar as a genre of both music and dance continued to develop throughout the twentieth century.

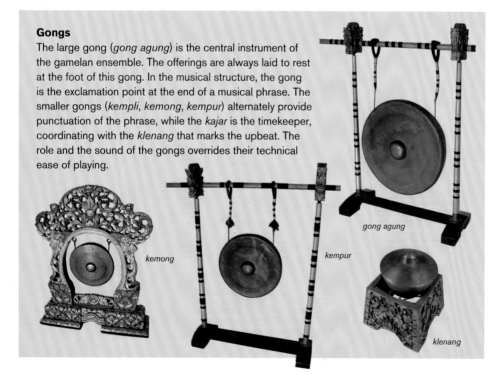

Gongs

The large gong (*gong agung*) is the central instrument of the gamelan ensemble. The offerings are always laid to rest at the foot of this gong. In the musical structure, the gong is the exclamation point at the end of a musical phrase. The smaller gongs (*kempli, kemong, kempur*) alternately provide punctuation of the phrase, while the *kajar* is the timekeeper, coordinating with the *klenang* that marks the upbeat. The role and the sound of the gongs overrides their technical ease of playing.

gong agung

kemong

kempur

klenang

In 1968, the first Gong Kebyar competition, called Mredangga Utsava, took place in Denpasar. The public began to favor new Kebyar compositions over the older, classical styles. The festival was repeated in 1969 and 1978, then annually from 1982 when it became a part of the Bali Arts Festival (Pesta Kesenian Bali) held at the Werdhi Budaya Art Centre. Each regency selects a group to represent that area and provides financial assistance. New compositions and dances are created and intense rehearsals occur for six months prior to the festival. Fierce competition takes place between the rival eight regencies and the municipality of Denpasar. The top four contenders present a program pitted against one of the other groups at the amphitheater in Denpasar. Great attention is paid to detail, from the costuming to the entrance of the musicians, to how they move their bodies as an ensemble. These are some of the most anticipated evenings of the Arts Festival. Loyal fans sit in sections behind their group and often hoot and holler, and even throw empty plastic water bottles at the rival ensemble to disturb their concentration. This is not the best forum to *hear* the music, but the excitement matches the energy of the music. To be one of the winners is a great honor and cassette tapes are made every year of the most acclaimed groups.

In 1985, a Festival Gong Wanita or Women's Gamelan Festival was started. This was replaced in 2001 with the first ever adult mixed group. Children's Kebyar groups have competed in the Festival since 1992 and are the pride and joy of each region.

A New Soundscape

One of the unique elements of Kebyar is the sound *byar*, when a number of notes are struck at the same time, creating a soundscape spanning octaves. The whole gamut of emotions is heard and felt. It is not music for meditation, but it certainly heightens the senses (and wakes one up!).

The *gender* (metallophones) of the shadow puppet play are more prominent in the Gong Kebyar because the keys of the *gender* are thinner than those of the *gangsa*, producing a more high-pitched sound. The abrupt starts and stops and complex rhythmic configurations allow a much wider range of expression. The older five-keyed *gangsa jongkok* now has nine or ten keys, affording a larger musical range.

Large *ceng-ceng* (cymbals) are replaced by smaller ones (*ricik*), and drum patterns are greatly altered by replacing slower stick drumming with much quicker and more exciting hand playing.

The tuning for Gong Kebyar is *saih lima* (five notes) in the *pelog* scale. Gong Kebyar can be grouped into three categories of size: *utama* is a full orchestra, *madya* is semi-complete; and *nista* has only half the instruments. A village can purchase a *nista* set and add to it as their coffers allow.

Kebyar music can be divided into styles from North and South Bali. North Balinese ensembles tend to play faster, with more complex ornamentation and sharper differentiation in rhythm. This style is less popular and now the style of South Bali is dominant.

In the past thirty years there has been great innovation in the musical world of Bali. With the advent of television, tourism and globalization, many new ideas and musical styles have come to the Balinese. The performing arts schools (SMKI and ISI) encourage their students to create new pieces (*kreasi baru*). Collaborations between Balinese and other Indonesians as well as foreigners are on the rise, and nearly every month some kind of fusion music or dance is performed on the island.

Carving gamelan stands in a pavilion. The holes are for the bamboo resonators. The artists carve directly onto the finished jackfruit wood stands.

Ida Bagus Sugatha of Griya Gunung Sari, Peliatan, playing the melodious two-stringed *rebab* or lute, the only stringed instrument in the gamelan.

The Full Ensemble

The following instruments comprise Gamelan Gong Kebyar, the most common gamelan ensemble in Bali.

two *gong agung*: large hanging gongs (80 cm in diameter)

one *kempur*: small hanging gong (55 cm in diameter)

one *kempli*: small hanging gong (35 cm in diameter)

one *kajar*: small horizontal gong (35 cm in diameter)

two *jegogan*: five keys, padded mallet

two *jublag* or *calung*: five keys, one octave higher than *jegogan*, padded mallet

two *penyacah*: seven keys, one octave higher than *jublag*, padded mallet

one or two *ugal*: ten keys, regular mallet, fifth note same as *penyacah*'s highest note

four *pemade*: ten keys, one octave higher than *ugal*, regular mallet

four *kantil*: ten keys, one octave higher than *pemade*, regular mallet

one *reyong*: twelve kettle gongs played by four musicians, each using two wooden sticks wrapped with cord on the ends

one *trompong*: ten kettle gongs, played by a soloist

two *kendang*: double-headed drums made out of *nangka* (jackfruit) wood hollowed out in an hourglass shape; heads are cow skin

one *ceng-ceng*: cymbals fastened onto a wooden base facing upwards and played with a hand-held pair facing down

ceng-ceng kopyak: pairs of hand-held crash cymbals

Tuning in the Gong Foundry

The actual tuning of the instruments is done at gamelan foundries located in a few villages, for example, Banjar Babakan in Blahbatuh (Gianyar); many in Tihingin (Klungkung); Denpasar (Banjar Abiankapas), and in Sawan (Buleleng). Here the smaller knobbed gongs and keys are forged. Large gongs are all made in Java. The metal, which is a bronze alloy (*kerawang*) of approximately ten parts tin to three parts copper, is melted in a crucible at extremely high heat and then poured into molds. Once the metal has solidified a bit, it is plunged into water and then reheated and shaped in a small fire of coconut shell chips which burn quickly at a very high temperature. After the key has obtained its desired shape, it is sent to the tuners and filers.

The tuner taps a key on the concrete floor to hear its pitch and then trims. The pitch is lowered by shaving off metal from the bottom. This makes the key longer in proportion to its thickness, causing it to vibrate more slowly when struck. To raise the pitch, the key is filed along one of the ends, shortening it to vibrate more quickly. Resonators used to be

gangsa kantil

gangsa pemade

kajar

ugal

kendang

made exclusively out of bamboo, but today many customers prefer longer lasting PVC piping. The pitch can be altered by changing the amount of space in the hollow of the bamboo or PVC tube. This is achieved by putting plugs into the tube at certain intervals.

Kettle gongs are forged in a similar fashion. First pounded into a flat circle, the sides and the knob are then beaten into shape. Tuner-filers are experts who can hear nuances in pitch even with all the clanging and banging around them. Two holes are drilled in each key which is then suspended in ascending order of pitch over the resonators.

The Cosmic Scale

The *lontar* script *Prakempa*, dating to the late eighteenth to mid-nineteenth centuries, refers to the mystical significance of the musical scale as having its roots in the *panca maha bhuta* ("five great elementals"): *pertiwi*, *bayu*, *apah*, *teja* and *akasa* (earth, wind, water, fire and ether). Each of these elements corresponds to one of the cardinal directions (plus center) and is associated with a deity, number, letter, color and sound. The creator of sound, Bhagawan

Wiswakarma, took sounds from all the directions and divided them into two five-note scales, *pelog* and *slendro*. *Pelog* is related to the Five Holy Waters and the God of Love, Semara; *slendro* is related to the Five Fires and the Goddess of Love, Ratih.

The large gong symbolizes heaven while the *kempur* (medium-sized gong) is the receptacle of all that is holy. The *kajar* (small timekeeping gong) is Guru, the Supreme Teacher who commands tempo. This is manifested in the microcosm within the musical structure. In the *lelambatan* (slow instrumental) piece "Tabuh Pat" (Song in Fours), there are four *kempur* and *kajar* strokes within one gong phrase. Each instrument corresponds to a part of the human body, and the path of sound in the body also is described in this treatise.

A gamelan without *ceng-ceng* cymbals is said to be like a meal without salt. The atonal interlocking rhythms spice up the songs.

jublag

gong agung

kempur

ceng-ceng

reyong

jegogan

Sacred and Ancient Ensembles

Almost all *gamelan tua* or ancient ensembles are tuned to a seven-tone *pelog* scale. Drums are not used. Their function is purely for ritual. What is deemed sacred depends on both the ensemble being played as well as its performance context. These ensembles are not as common as the Kebyar ensemble and you are lucky if you catch one of them in a ceremony. The ethereal sounds played on iron, bamboo and bronze keys will transport you back in time.

Gamelan Selonding players in Mengwi. An ancient type of gamelan, the Selonding used to be known only in the Bali Aga villages of East and North Bali but is now being introduced outside of its traditional realm.

The Meaning of Sacred Gamelan

There is a misconception among visitors to Bali that all music and dance is "sacred" or deemed "temple music and dance." While every kind of gamelan music may be performed during temple or family rituals, some ensembles are considered more sacred than others for several reasons. They are performed in the *jeroan*, the inner and most sacred courtyard of the temple, they are relatively obscure, and they first appeared prior to the fifteenth century (see p. 22).

These ensembles are not taken out of their storage spaces without offerings and new pieces are not composed for them in their ritual context. However, young composers today are indeed making new music for old ensembles (see p. 102). All of these ensembles utilize a seven-tone *pelog* scale and are glossed as part of the "ancient" category of gamelan.

The Iron-Keyed Gamelan Selonding

Gamelan Selonding is found predominantly in Bali Aga (aboriginal) villages, mainly in the Karangasem district of East Bali, although it is gaining popularity throughout the island. This is a seven-tone *pelog* (Eb, F, G, Ab, Bb, C, D) iron ensemble used only in a ritual setting. The power of this gamelan is so great that it is said the playing of it can harmonize the spiritual well-being of the village. One of the distinguishing features of this gamelan is that it is played with two wooden mallets, one in each hand. The iron keys are placed over a roughly hewn wooden soundbox, four keys to a soundbox. Each instrument has eight keys or two soundboxes. There is no *kotekan* or interlocking rhythms, just a haunting and melodious timbre. The ensemble includes five eight-keyed metallophones played by eight musicians.

Gamelan Gong Gede

The largest gamelan ensemble, Gamelan Gong Gede (literally "great gamelan"), has nearly sixty players. It consists of a number of *gangsa jongkok* (metallophones with one large resonating chamber), metallophones, gongs, cymbals and drums. Solos are performed on the twelve-note *trompong* (kettle gong chime) and elaborations on the *reyong* (four-note kettle gong). The five-tone *pelog* scale supports extra *calung*, *jegogan*, and *gangsa* (metallophones with individually tuned resonators). The music is slow and dignified, and in a word, great. Its repertoire includes *lelambatan*, ceremonial gamelan pieces heard at all temple festivals. Gong Gede also accompanies ritual Baris dances. Nowadays, young Balinese composers also use some of the instruments to play contemporary compositions. It is found in Bangli, Gianyar and Denpasar.

One of the better known Gamelan Gong Gede ensembles comes from the village of Kintamani, Batur. This group performs at the temple ceremonies at Pura Ulun Danu in Batur.

In Tenganan Pegeringsingan, the villagers say that long ago they heard the sounds of thunder from the sky. The first thunderclap fell to the earth at Bongaya and the second at Tenganan Pegeringsingan. Sets of *selonding* appeared where the thunder hit. These are only taken out and played during the twice-yearly rituals (usually in January–February and June–July) in Tenganan Pegeringsingan. In the 1980s, ISI (Indonesian Arts Institute) made copies of this sacred ensemble so that students could learn on it. Gamelan Selonding can also be heard in the mountain village of Kayubii, Kintamani.

The Bronze-Keyed Gamelan Gong Luang

This is another ensemble used for rituals. It is a seven-tone *pelog* scaled ensemble that consists of nine different types of instruments played by 10–20 musicians. These include various sized *saron* (thick bronze keys over a trough), a *gambang* (xylophone), two *jegogan* (metallophones), one *trompong* or *reyong* (rack of inverted kettle gongs), two large gongs, one *kempur* (medium-sized gong), 2–4 pairs of medium-sized cymbals (*ceng-ceng kopyak*), *gangsa* (metallophones), and two *kendang* (drums). The number and types of instruments varies from village to village. This is a bronze gamelan except for the *gambang* which consists of bamboo keys over a wooden soundbox.

Gamelan Gong Luang is used to complete ceremonial needs, accompany dance (Topeng, Baris Poleng, Pendet and Rejang) and to to fulfill a vow (*mayah sesangi*). In Dewa Yadnya (temple festivals), Gamelan Gong Luang music is part of the ritual, although not all the instruments are used, the *saron* for example. For cremations, the same holds true. For the purification rites following cremation (*memukur* or *maligiya*), the whole gamelan, including the *saron*, is used.

The music played on the Gong Luang ensemble is melodic. It is colored by elaborations of the *gambang* and *reyong* and with accents by the *saron* and *jegogan*. One of the unique features of the ensemble is its sixteen-pot *trompong*; four musicians sit in two rows facing each other to play this instrument. The gamelan has a serene sound unlike other ensembles, and evokes a time long ago. It can be seen in only a few villages today in Bali, including Singapadu (Gianyar), Tangkas (Klungkung) Krobokan (Badung) and Kesiut (Tabanan).

Gamelan Gong Bheri and the Baris Cina Dance

Gong Bheri is probably one of the most rarely heard ensembles and can only be found in Renon and Semawang in Sanur. The instruments are made of bronze. The ensemble consists of two flat gongs, *klenteng* (a higher pitched small gong), two *tawa-tawa* (small knobbed gongs), *bebende* (large gong), *kajar* (small knobbed gong) *kempli* (small flat gong), *klenang* (small flat gong), *sangka* (conch shell), a set of *ceng-ceng* (cymbals) and *bedug* (barrel-shaped drum). Since the *bedug* is a type of drum used in the mosque, it is thought that this ensemble came to Bali from Java. It was originally housed in Renon but frequently moved. In each new location it claimed a human victim every time it was played.

Gong Bheri is used to accompany the Baris Cina dance. Both costume and name indicate Chinese influence. The dance depicts two platoons of nine soldiers, one dressed in white, the other in black. It is only performed when someone in the village makes a vow to the temple and sponsors the dance in order to effect a cure. The enormous quantity of offerings involved makes the cost prohibitive. The dance is rarely performed and only in Renon and Sanur.

Gamelan Gambang and Gamelan Caruk

Gamelan Gambang accompanies religious rituals such as cremations in North, Central and South Bali and temple festivals in East Bali. It is a seven-tone *pelog* scaled ensemble with six instruments. Four of these instruments are made out of fourteen bamboo keys and are played by one musician holding two double-headed mallets. The other two instruments are bronze *saron*. The resonating box for the *saron* is quite small and the keys are placed on top of this box as opposed to being suspended over a bamboo tube, which changes the sound substantially. Gamelan Gambang is performed in Tenganan, Asak, Bebandem (Karangasem), Singapadu, Perangsada, Saba, Sukawati, Blahbatuh (Gianyar), Kesiut (Tabanan), Kerobakan, Sempidi, Kapal and Manikliyu (Badung), and Jirengdalem (Buleleng).

An extremely rare ensemble called Caruk consists of two *gambang* and one *saron*, all of them smaller in size than the regular Gamelan Gambang. This is performed only at cremation rites in Bebandem, Saba, Dharmasada, Krobokan, Sempidi and Abiansemal.

Gamelan Gambang is a wooden gamelan ensemble in which the keys of the *gambang* instruments are placed over a soundbox. Four notes can be struck an octave apart. The left and right hand mallets strike at different times, creating interlocking rhythms with the other *gambang*. This type of ensemble demands highly skilled musicians who usually specialize only in *gambang*.

Ceremonial Marching Gamelans

A marching gamelan is an almost daily occurrence in Bali. It accompanies images of deities which are moved, along with offerings, from one sacred place to another, cremation of the dead, and ritual bathing of the gods. The rhythms keep worshippers in step with the procession and add to the feeling of *ramai* (festiveness). A lighter and more portable gamelan is needed, such as the melodious Gamelan Angklung or the boisterous Gamelan Balaganjur.

Drums and cymbals play a percussive beat in this marching gamelan, known as Gamelan Balaganjur. The ensemble is taking part in a temple ceremony.

Small, suspended metallophones characterize this Gamelan Angklung, making its way to a cremation ceremony.

Gamelan Angklung, Sweet Melancholy

Grouped in the *tua* (ancient) category, the small Gamelan Angklung is portable and thus easy to carry in processions. The instruments hang from bamboo poles carried on the shoulders of two men with a third person playing from behind. To a Balinese, the sweet sounds of the Angklung are melancholic and carry a tinge of sadness, so it is used for cremation ceremonies in many parts of Bali. Yet to the outsider it has a "sparkling" sound. Nearly every village has at least one Angklung ensemble. It requires fewer players (18) than the larger ensembles (25–30).

The only ensemble with a four-note *slendro* scale (such as G#, A#, C, D# and E, F#, A, B—although North Bali uses five notes), Gamelan Angklung mainly plays a classical repertoire in keeping with the ritual and religious ceremonies for which it is primarily

used. Gong Kebyar Angklung accompanies Kebyar dances with a repertoire fashioned after Gong Kebyar (see pp. 24–5).

The instruments in the Gamelan Angklung are the smallest on the island. The ensemble consists of 5–7 sets of *gangsa* (metallophones) of differing sizes, two *jegogan* (larger metallophones), four paired sets of *reyong* (kettle gongs), a pair of drums, a gong, one each of the *tawa-tawa* (small kettle gong), *kemong* (medium-sized gong) and *klenang* (small gong), *ceng-ceng* (cymbals), and several *suling* (end-blown flutes). *Gangsa* play the most important role, starting the melody and elaborating on the compositions.

Denpasar has some of the best Angklung groups on the island, and these can be found in Banjars Lebah, Taensiat, Kayu Mas, Bengkel and Titih. Elsewhere, they exist in Sidan, Peliatan, Pejeng and Sukawati (Gianyar), Sukasada (Bungkulan), Kamasan (Klungkung), Kintamani (Bangli), Selat (Karangasem) and Tejakula (Buleleng).

Gamelan Balaganjur, Marching to the Beat

Balaganjur ("to excite an army") is a traditional gamelan used to accompany processions for cremations and temple festivals. The music is extremely percussive. Sometimes this ensemble is called Gamelan Kalaganjur ("to excite demons") when played in a sitting position to accompany demon-appeasing rites (*mecaru*). Each regency has different variations of technique and instruments.

The basic instruments are 8–10 sets of large crash cymbals (*ceng-ceng kopyak*), six *reyong* pots, two gongs, one each of the *kempur* (medium-sized gong), *bebende* (smaller flat gong), *kajar* (timekeeping flat gong), *tawa-tawa*, and two large drums. The melody is provided by the *reyong* and rhythmic elaborations of the *ceng-ceng* played in interlocking configurations. Usually 25–30 musicians play and carry the instruments while marching in a procession or sitting at the festival venue or cremation site.

Other Forms of Balaganjur

Other variations of Gamelan Balaganjur exist in Bali. **Gamelan Tambur** has one large drum and one gong but no *reyong*. The *ceng-ceng* still have a big role and are played in interlocking rhythms. **Gamelan Bebonangan** uses only a few sets of *ceng-ceng*, one drum and one gong, usually to accompany cremations in North and East Bali.

In the past two decades, there has been a renewed interest among young men in this type of music. In some cases, fierce rivalry has been channeled into competitions for the "best" Gamelan Balaganjur.

Numerous competitive events now take place. Best known is the annual Ogoh-Ogah festival on the day before Nyepi (Day of Silence). Large papier-mâché demon figures (*ogoh-ogoh*) are carried through the streets accompanied by Gamelan Balaganjur. The musicians play as loud and boisterously as possible to scare the invisible demons away. The demons then go back to their other island residence and leave the Balinese in peace. The *ogoh-ogoh* are then burned, symbolizing their banishment. The following day, Nyepi, the island is virtually silent since any kind of entertainment, work, or travel is prohibited.

To welcome the new millennium, tens of marching Gamelan Balaganjur players strutted their stuff in downtown Denpasar on the eve of the New Year.

Gamelan Semar Pagulingan and Gamelan Pelegongan

These two ensembles are very similar in sound and instrumentation. There is a delicate sweetness that inspires romance and the graceful movements of the Legong dance. Physically, the instruments are smaller, especially the gongs; the one-mallet *gangsa* metallophone is replaced by 2–4 two-mallet *gender*, rendering a lightness in tone. There is a return to composing for the seven-tone Semar Pagulingan although there still are not many ensembles left in Bali.

Gender rambat are particular to Gamelan Semar Pagulingan. They are played with two mallets instead of the regular one. This lends the music a characteristic fluidity.

The Sweet Sounds of Love

Probably the sweetest music comes from the Semar Pagulingan ensemble, named from the Kawi (old Javanese) word for "sleeping" (*a guling*). This ensemble would accompany the king and his consort making love in the sleeping chambers. Its ethereal sound uses a seven-note, rather than the more standard five-note, *pelog* scale. Much of the repertoire originates from Gambuh music.

The instruments include several paired metallophones (*kantil, pemade, gender barangan, gender rambat, jublag, jegog*), *trompong* (kettle gong chime), *kemong* and *klenang* (smaller gongs), *kajar* (small timekeeping gong), *ricik* (cymbals), *gentorag* (bell tree), *rebab* (bowed lute), several *suling* (bamboo flutes), and two *kendang* (drums). The *trompong* is the melodic leader, with the drums controlling the dynamics and changes of tempo. *Suling* melodies are transformed into ethereal and elaborate configurations by the fourteen kettles of the imposing *trompong*—all played by the one musician!

The sweetness of this gamelan is due to several factors, mainly instrument and scale changes. There is no *reyong*, an instrument similar to the *trompong*, but played by four people. Small *ricik* cymbals are used instead of the larger *ceng-ceng*. The *kemong* (medium-size gong) replaces the large gong. Four *gender* are used instead of larger *gangsa*. The delicate sound of these instruments, used to play the core melody, enriches the music. *Gender* musicians use two mallets with wooden disks at the ends.

The few Semar Pagulingan ensembles still active in Bali can be found in the villages of Peliatan (Tirta Sari group in Banjar Taruna) and Kamasan (Klungkung), and in Banjars Pagan Kelod and Sesetan Kaja (Denpasar) and Sempidi (Badung). The newer Semara Dhana is a combination of Semar Pagulingan and Gong Kebyar, but still cannot match the ethereal sounds of Gamelan Semar Pagulingan.

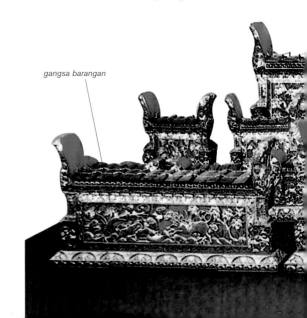

gangsa barangan

Gamelan Pelegongan

Gamelan Pelegongan is a fraternal twin of Semar Pagulingan, except that it utilizes a five-tone *pelog* scale. One set of *gender* are pitched an octave higher than the other. The two drums are slightly smaller. As this gamelan usually accompanies the classical Legong dance, the music is filled with dynamic shifts in tempo and elaborate configurations played on the higher-pitched metallophones. The drummers have much more freedom to play intricate, highly paced patterns. There are many *angsel* (changes in tempo) or rests. Since the theater forms Calonarang and Barong-Rangda are accompanied by this ensemble, it also is known as Gamelan Bebarongan.

A composition begins with an introduction by the larger pair of *gender*, played in octaves. The skill of the musicians shows in the quick hand work; each hand breaks away from the other to play either a variation of the melody or the interlocking rhythms.

The colotomic structure in this music differs from Gamelan Gong Gede and Gamelan Gong Kebyar. The gongs are, in order of size, *kempur*, *kemong*, *kajar* and *klenang*. The *kempur* and *kemong* play in alteration at more frequent intervals. The *kajar*, as the timekeeper, plays on

The medium-sized Gamelan Pelegongan, played by twenty musicians, accompanies Legong dances as well as Barong and Calonarang dance-dramas. Normally, Gamelan Pelegongan uses two small drums but some groups, such as the one shown here, use medium-sized drums (*kerumpungan*).

the beat but with elaborations made by hitting the boss (knob) as well as the flat surface. These produce two entirely different sounds. The *klenang* plays on the offbeats.

Gamelan Pelegongan are found in all parts of the island. Some of the better known ones are in Tista Kerambitan and Tunjuk (Tabanan), Teges Kanginan (Peliatan), Ketewel and Saba (Gianyar), Bengkel and Binoh (Denpasar). Each village uses a different tuning mode based on the local taste.

A Gamelan Semar Pagulingan. It is usual for the drums, *gender rambat*, *kajar* and *kempur* to be positioned in the center of this ensemble so that they can be heard by the other players.

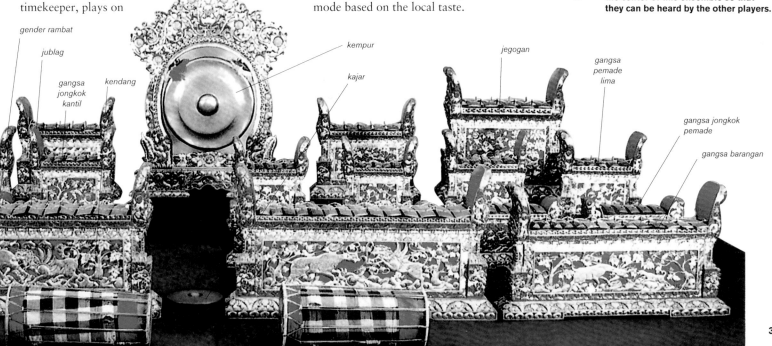

gender rambat
jublag
gangsa jongkok kantil
kendang
kempur
kajar
jegogan
gangsa pemade lima
gangsa jongkok pemade
gangsa barangan

Bamboo Ensembles

It is no surprise that many musical ensembles in Bali are made out of bamboo. Quick growing, light and easy to cut, bamboo is a renewable resource and inexpensive, making it the ideal material for the music of the masses. Bamboo ensembles can be categorized into three types: tuned bamboo bars or tubes (Grantang, Jegog and Rindik, collectively called Bumbung Tingklik), stamping tubes (Gebyog) and bamboo slit drums (Tektekan, Bumbang).

The *suling*, or Balinese end-blown flute, utilizes circular breathing. *Suling* are an integral part of many Balinese gamelans.

The instruments in the foreground of this ensemble are made out of bamboo tubes and are called *tingklik*. They are played with two mallets. Nowadays, it is common for women to play *tingklik*.

Gamelan Grantang

Gamelan Grantang is perhaps the best known bamboo ensemble throughout Bali. This five-note *slendro* ensemble accompanies a social dance known as Joged Bumbung (see pp. 86–7). In Buleleng, there is a five-tone ensemble known as Grantang Pelog which also accompanies Joged Bumbung. This gamelan is named after the *bumbung* (bamboo tubes) used for the instruments, which are lashed together and hung in a frame. There are 6–8 *grantang* (bamboo xylophones) of different sizes, 3–4 pairs of *kepyak* (split bamboo tubes), *gong pulu* (gong), *ceng-ceng* (cymbals), *kajar* (timekeeping gong), *tawa-tawa* (small gong), 3–5 small *suling* (end-blown bamboo flutes), and one *kendang* (drum). All *grantang* players use two mallets with a rubber disk at the ends; the right hand plays the interlocking rhythms and the left hand plays the bass and basic melody. In South Central Bali, some groups include *reyong* (kettle gongs) and *jegogan* (large metallophones) in the ensemble.

Gamelan Rindik

The five-note *pelog* Gamelan Rindik is used to accompany the social dance Joged Pingitan or Joged Gandrangan (see p. 87). The social dance Gandrung uses this ensemble so it is also known as Gamelan Gandrung. The instruments include four pairs of *tingklik* (bamboo xylophones), *gong pulu*, *kajar*, *ceng-ceng*, *suling* and one drum. The music is upbeat and lively. This ensemble is not as common as Gamelan Grantang but can be found in Pekuwudan in Sukawati and Tegunungan in Blahbatuh (Gianyar), Ketapian (Denpasar), Sibang Gede, Tangeb and Munggu (Badung).

Gong Suling

This flute-dominated five-note *pelog* ensemble emerged in the 1950s. Most Gong Suling music comes from the Kebyar repertoire with the *gangsa* (metallophone) parts played by 25–30 *suling*. The ensemble is little seen today.

Roaring Thunder of Gamelan Jegog

Gamelan Jegog is the only four-tone *pelog* ensemble on the island and consists of big and long bamboo xylophones. Jegog is perhaps the biggest bamboo ensemble in the world and is named after the largest instrument, the *jegog*. This gamelan is traditionally found only in the regency of Jembrana, West Bali. The ensemble is composed of six groups of bamboo xylophones, from the largest to the smallest *jegog*, *undir*, *suir*, *celuluk*, *kancil* and *barangan*. Each has eight bamboo tubes, the largest of which is 3 meters long. Two *kendang* (drums), *tawa-tawa* (small gong), and a large *rebana* (circular frame drum) may be added when accompanying martial arts dances. A character called Dag improvises his dance while directing the musicians and dancers (see p. 89). He wears a costume reminiscent of the Middle East, reflecting a more prevalent Muslim influence in Jembrana than in other parts of Bali.

The sound of this gamelan is said to be like "roaring thunder" and, indeed, when two Jegog groups play against one another (*mebarung*), the earth shakes. In the past, Jegog was performed to indicate that a festival or other special event was about to happen. Today, it plays at village festivals such as Mekepung (bull race) and also accompanies Kebyar dances. There are sixty groups, primarily in the districts of Negara and Mendoyo.

Sounding out a tune on these instruments takes a a great deal of strength and stamina. The large bamboo tubes are struck with two mallets. The larger instruments feature bamboo so broad that the musicians actually sit on the instrument to play them.

Bumbung Gebyog

Bumbung Gebyog is a small ensemble from West Bali featuring bamboo stamping tubes. Played among farmers, Gebyog is usually performed by a group of women expressing their joy after a rice harvest. It is also played to signal family ceremonies taking place, and may be used to accompany Joged Bumbung.

The ensemble has 8–12 *gebyog* made from *tiing buluh*, bamboo which is thin and sturdy. Each piece is played by one person, who stamps the *gebyog* on a piece of wood to create interlocking configurations. In many ways, the patterns of *gebyog* are reminiscent of the syncopated rice pounding rhythms (*oncang-oncangan*) used traditionally when husking Balinese rice. Only a few groups remain in the Negara regency.

Tektekan

This is a large bamboo ensemble with around 100 bamboo *kulkul* (slit-drums). Originally Tektekan was played for exorcism rites when an epidemic hit the village; it is now played to accompany the Calonarang dance-drama in the Tabanan regency. The music is characterized by multiple layers of interlocking rhythms similar to the Kecak, or the rhythms of large *ceng-ceng kopyak* (cymbals) in Balaganjur. This ensemble is completed with *kajar*, *kemong*, *klenang* (gongs), *ceng-ceng* (cymbals) and a *kendang* (drum). Today it is found in Kerambitan and Kediri.

Bumbang

This recent innovation was created by the late I Nyoman Rembang, who was famous for his compositions and for making bamboo instruments. The word derives from a combination of "bumbung by Rembang." He made this music to accompany a new dance piece about a school of fish for the Bali Arts Festival in 1982. The ensemble is dominated by *bumbang* (tuned bamboo tubes) of all sizes played by about fifty musicians. Each person strikes one or two bamboo tubes with mallets. A gong, *ceng-ceng*, flutes and drums are also included. The music is more melodious than rhythmic.

A bamboo *kajar* from the rare Gamelan Leko. In this ensemble, the *kajar* player strikes a unique pattern of three down- and off-beats.

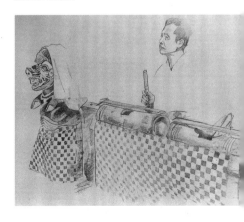

Women in Non-Traditional Roles

Before the early 1980s, one would be hard pressed to find a female musician or *dalang* (puppeteer). The role of women in Bali is traditionally one of housekeeper and mother and they have little leisure time to pursue other interests. The 1980s brought much change in the artistic world, with collaborations and meetings between performing artists from all over the world. Women were seen as a viable creative force and female gamelan musicians and puppeteers are becoming more common as their new artistic roles are given more credibility.

Gender roles in Bali are closely defined and delineated. The patriarchal culture ensures that women conform to expectations. Aside from regular household duties, women spend a great amount of time making temple offerings and in ritual activities. They do not have a lot of leisure time, and this is a problem in sustaining women's gamelan groups. *Sekaa* (gamelan clubs) are usually associated with the *banjar* (hamlet). A multitude of ritual obligations take precedence over rehearsals and interest may wane.

Different Learning Styles

Young boys are encouraged to get outside, go to their friends' homes, and hang out at the *bale banjar* (community hall) where the gamelan instruments are kept.

Women's gamelan competitions are becoming more and more common. This group is from Gemeh, Denpasar.

Little girls, on the other hand, are expected to stay close to home, helping their female relatives with cooking and making offerings. When children grow up, they still conform to these roles. Males of all ages tend to congregate at the *bale banjar* to play gamelan, and children bang on the instruments when not in use by the adults. Young women do not go out at night alone, nor are they encouraged to play gamelan.

First Notes

In the early 1960s, girls at KOKAR (High School of Performing Arts) studied gamelan as part of their curriculum. The seeds were thus planted. The first *gamelan wanita* (women's gamelan) was started by Ni Ketut Suryatini, a musician and composer in her own right. Born into a family of musicians and instrument makers in Kayumas, Denpasar, she was used to performing with her male relatives. The group Puspasari was founded in 1980 by Suryatini and her brother I Wayan Suweca. This group of women performed on local television, sparking so much interest that every regency started its own *gamelan wanita*.

Desak Suarti Laksmi, also of Denpasar, became the first female to teach gamelan abroad and has composed numerous pieces. Mekar Ayu was started in Pengosekan village in 1993 by Desak Nyoman Suarti and Ni Gusti Putu Astiti to give the women a chance to perform and to acquire self-esteem. Later, this group worked with Topeng Sakti, the only women's Topeng group. One of the drummers for this group, Ni Wayan Mudiari (Kocan), is now teaching teenage and children's groups in Denpasar. Suarti formed a new group, Luh Luwih, in 1995 who perform an all-women's Calonarang and Kecak, among other forms. Other groups which have continued over the years are in Lembongan, Nusa Penida (Klungkung), Sebatu and Peliatan (Gianyar) and Perean (Tabanan).

In 1985, the women's group Mekar Sari of Peliatan, a village renowned for its musicians and dancers, began practicing a few times a week under the tutelage of Anak Agung Gede Mandera. In the beginning, they did not take themselves seriously as musicians. However, after a period of time they were ready to make their debut. Now they perform every Sunday for tourists, accompanying children doing animal and other dances.

In some villages, the women faced opposition from their families, in particular their husbands. Since the women dressed up for the show and performed at night, the husbands suspected they might start having affairs. In one village, the men's gamelan group became jealous of the women's group which was being invited to perform more frequently than they were. They finally forbade the women to perform. Yet there are other villages where the men are extremely proud of their *gamelan wanita* and more groups are appearing today. In the cities, groups associated with government agencies and Women's Auxiliary Groups (Dharma Wanita) start their own *gamelan wanita* to perform for official functions.

Many of these musicians are former dancers who, after getting married, ceased performing because they were taking care of children, their husbands would not allow them to continue, or they were embarrassed to go on stage. Playing gamelan is one outlet whereby their creativity can be challenged, and more importantly, a way in which they can *ngayah* (perform devotional work) for the temple. Temple ceremonial *lelambatan* music, which is smooth and mellow, is said to be more appropriate to women's energy. These pieces do not require as much rehearsal as the more flashy Kebyar ones and therefore are easier to learn.

In 1985, women's gamelan groups started to participate in the Bali Arts Festival. Each of the eight regencies sent one group to represent them, and there was fierce competition and equally fierce pride in these first women's groups. They were met with comments such as "How can they use the mallets when their breasts get in the way?" and "Ah, no way a woman can play the drum." The women, who are expected to conform to Balinese ideas of femininity, were told to sit with their legs tucked under them and play the drum on a stand instead of in their laps. It was almost impossible to play that way, so their solution was to wear their *kain* (skirts) more loosely wrapped to facilitate sitting cross-legged.

The Luh Luwih troupe began performing the masked *Ramayana* form of Wayang Wong in 2002. This was the first time that an all-women's Wayang Wong troupe had performed in Bali.

Now that *gamelan wanita* are seen in tourist venues, on television and at local temple festivals, they are gaining more acceptance. There are even exclusively female Gamelan Balaganjur, a real deviation from the norm, as this music is loud, crashing and "masculine." The appearance of the American group Gamelan Sekar Jaya (see p. 103) on Indonesian television showed the Balinese that both men and women could play music. Nearly every village now vies to have their own *gamelan wanita*.

Women as Dalang

The art of puppetry has been confined to men for centuries, but recently a number of women have established themselves as *dalang* in their own right. The stories and puppets remain the same; this is not a new women's art. In the 1970s, after spending time in the United States and teaching puppetry to Westerners (including the female director Julie Taymor), I Nyoman Sumandhi returned to Bali and began to teach women puppetry, including at the High School of Performing Arts (SMKI). In 1980, the first competition for women *dalang* in Bali was held: Ni Ketut Trijata (granddaughter of the famous I Retug) from Tunjuk came in first, while second place winner was Ni Ketut Nondri, widow of one of Bali's favorite *dalang*, the late I Ketut Madra, and sister of *dalang* I Wayan Wija. Ni Nyoman Canderi, a very well-known Arja dancer, occasionally does Wayang Arja. Yet again, due to the ritual calendar, the incredible energy expended at every show, and the late performance hours, female *dalang* are still a tiny minority.

The clashing of cymbals and beating of drums is usually reserved for the men's club, but here in Medangan, Gianyar, this women's Balaganjur group plays at a Barong festival.

Children's Gamelan and Dance Groups

Their heads barely visible over the tops of the instruments, one would think of children's gamelan groups as "cute." Far from it. The maturity of their playing is astonishing; the expressiveness and stamina of the dancers amazing. Meeting 2–3 times a week, these "clubs of small people" study seriously and the cream of the crop end up representing their regency in the Bali Arts Festival. Their teachers and parents hope that by planting the seed of creativity and teamwork in their children at an early age, they will grow up to be great artists.

Beginning of Children's Sekaa

In 1937, the Canadian musicologist and Bali resident Colin McPhee organized the first children's gamelan group. Having studied Balinese music for years, he wanted to see if children—who normally did not play music—would begin to play if left to their own devices and with access to instruments. A serious group of what he called "small men," boys 6–11, gathered in his house. Prior to this, only grown men played gamelan. This first children's group in Banjar Kutuh, Sayan, continued until the "small men" became big.

Children as musicians were not taken seriously by the Balinese until the 1960s. Adults never thought a full children's gamelan group could be successful because of the children's supposedly short attention span. However, the children came through with flying colors and now there are children's groups everywhere. Since 1998, the annual Bali Arts Festival has featured a children's gamelan category. For the most part, these groups are still confined to small men rather than small women. The seriousness of these youngsters is a delight to experience.

In the Bali Aga village of Tenganan, children begin learning dance at a very early age. This Rejang, in which the females dress in their finest *geringsing* ikat clothing, is usually danced in the months of January and June.

I Putu Agustana playing the *trompong* at a contest in Denpasar. Competitions for Kebyar Trompong are held all over the island.

Of the many children's groups, one of the oldest is Warini in East Denpasar. Started by Ni Ketut Arini Alit in 1974, it was named after her uncle, I Wayan Rindi, a star dancer in the 1920s. This was originally his *sanggar* (dance studio), but when he became too busy he turned it over to Arini. Warini has produced thousands of dancers and musicians over the years. Arini's premise is that if children are given encouragement and a solid grounding, they will be able to learn new pieces with ease.

Students pay Rp 10,000 (US $1) a month and may take classes 2–4 times a week. Beginning students, numbering over a hundred, learn at her home on Saturday afternoons and Sunday mornings. There is a progression of skill level; more advanced students study after school during the week or privately. Once a year, on the anniversary of the *sanggar* (5 January), students are tested with a public performance in full costume at the Taman Budaya Art Centre.

Probably the most unique *sanggar* on the island is Bajra Sandi, started by Ida Wayan Oka Granoka of Budakeling, Karangasem, in 1991. A lecturer in Balinese literature at Udayana University, he resides and teaches in Denpasar. His philosophy is that everything stems from *sastra* (literature) and all of the *sanggar* members should know how it relates to dance and music. This *sanggar* is one of the few to have both girls and boys in the same group, and girls are given prominent roles as musicians and dancers. The children are encouraged to perform as both musicians and dancers in the same piece. Granoka instills a sense of propriety in his students and they do no commercial performances. They perform for cremations and temple ceremonies or for civic entertainment. Granoka and his family create pieces based on Gambuh and Legong movements and music. They also perform with two Barong and Rangda masks. "Prabasuara" (Dawning of a New World) had the dancers recreating on the dance floor the path that the breath takes in the body. In 2004, they represented Indonesia in the Cultural Olympics in Athens.

At the Agung Rai Museum of Art (ARMA) in Pengosekan, Ubud, children may study daily free of charge in the Sanggar ARMA Kumara Sari. Anak Agung Gede Rai, owner of the museum, encourages community participation and use of the museum facilities. He has made available a gamelan, rehearsal and

performance space, as well as inviting highly qualified teachers from his home village of Peliatan, a center of dance and music. Agung Rai wishes to preserve the special local style. The children perform every Saturday night at the museum and at local temple festivals. They were winners in the 1999 Bali Arts Festival Children's Gamelan competition, and in 2001 represented Bali in the National Children's Day in Jakarta.

Also in Pengosekan village is Sanggar Çudamani, founded in 1997 by Dewa Putu Berata. Çudamani has five gamelan groups: an adult male group, an adult women's group, a girls' group, a teenage boys' group (also winners in the 1999 Bali Arts Festival children's competition), and a young boys' group. All five of these groups perform at local temple festivals.

One of Çudamani's goals is to preserve the old classical music and dance pieces as well as collaborate with other artists to create innovative works. One of their signature pieces is Wayang Listrik (Electric Wayang), a new form of shadow puppetry (see p. 49).

All of these groups welcome visitors but it is best to call first to ensure that rehearsals are taking place, as school commitments and rituals take precedence (see p. 104).

Student dancers at ARMA in Peliatan, Ubud. Dance classes take place on a regular basis for the local children at the ARMA Museum.

During the Galungan holidays, one can often see children's Barong groups parading around the streets.

The Stories in Balinese Theater

The Indian epics *Ramayana* and *Mahabharata* are rich sources of stories for Balinese theater. The great king Rama, his wife Sita and younger brother Laksmana fight alongside Hanuman, the Monkey General, against the unsavory Rawana. In the *Mahabharata*, two sets of cousins vie for the crown in a tremendous war. Balinese and Javanese chronicles, romances, legends and fables, as well as stories from China, are also important sources for storytelling.

Reading of a *lontar* (palm leaf book) at post-cremation purification rites at Gianyar, 1992. The reading of sacred texts (*pesantian*) and their interpretation is conducted at many types of rituals. These palm leaf books are held in great respect by the Balinese as they contain knowledge which has been passed on from generation to generation.

Right: Rama and Sugriwa in Wayang Wong at Yayasan Tejakukus, Tejakula, Buleleng, 1995. This is the meeting scene between King Rama and the Monkey General Sugriwa in their preparations to cross the ocean to attack Rawana.

Clowns provide comic relief in the Barong dance-drama. These clowns spend the night in the cemetery to guard the newly dug graves of children. During the night, they will be visited by Celuluk, a nymphomaniac witch in training.

Balinese dance and theater draw their stories (called *satwa*) from six main sources: the famous Indian epics *Ramayana* and *Mahabharata*, the *Babad* or Balinese Chronicles of Kings, the *Malat* or *Panji* romances, the semi-historical East Javanese *Calonarang* exorcistic legend and the Javanese-Balinese fables, *Tantri*. In performance, all stories are improvised through dance, dialog and narration.

Ramayana

Attributed to the sage Valmiki, the *Ramayana* was written around the fourth century BCE. There are traditionally seven sections (*kanda*) from which episodes are re-enacted. "Bala Kanda" tells of Rama and his younger brother Laksmana as youths when they go into the forest to destroy the ogre Marica and his followers, who have disturbed a hermit-priest's meditation. After killing the ogres, Rama wins the hand of Sita in a royal archery contest.

The second part, "Ayodya Kandha," describes the tragedy at Ayodya palace. King Dasaratha's third wife, Kekayi, wants her son Bharata to become king of Ayodya. She convinces her husband to banish Rama, the rightful heir, his wife Sita and brother Laksmana to twelve years of exile in the forest. During their exile, King Dasaratha passes away.

The Abduction of Sita

"Aranya Kanda" tells of the abduction of Sita by the ogre-king Rawana. A golden deer, actually the ogre Marica in disguise, entices Sita. She implores her husband to catch the deer for her. Reluctantly, Rama leaves his wife in his brother's care. Shortly after, they hear Rama's cry for help. Laksmana is sure it is a trick, but Sita insists he go after his older brother. Before leaving Sita, he draws a magic circle around her for protection. An itinerant mendicant, ogre-king Rawana in disguise, approaches Sita begging for alms. When she steps out of the circle to give him some food, he snatches her up and flies away to Alengka. Rawana is attacked by the giant bird Jatayu, faithful ally of King Dasaratha, but Rawana cuts his wings. Jatayu falls to earth, but before dying tells Rama what has transpired.

Subali and Sugriwa, the Monkey Brothers

"Kiskenda Kanda" describes two monkey brothers, Subali and Sugriwa, battling the demon Mahesasura, who lives in Kiskenda cave. During the fight, Sugriwa believes that Subali has been killed by the ogre-king, so he seals the cave with a large rock. Subali manages to escape and seeks revenge

on Sugriwa, whom he believes trapped him in order to wed his wife, Dewi Tara. With Rama's help, Sugriwa destroys his brother. In return, Sugriwa lends Rama his monkey armies to rescue Sita from Rawana and to regain his throne.

"Sundara Kanda" depicts Rama sending the monkey commander Hanuman to Alengka to locate Sita. After overcoming many obstacles, he finds Sita and gives her Rama's ring, proving he is an ally. Sita, in turn, hands him a golden flower from her hair to show Rama that they have met. Before leaving Alengka, Hanuman destroys Rawana's palace garden and sets the city aflame.

"Yudha Kandha" tells of the bloody battle between Rama and Rawana with massive death and destruction of the ogres. Rama finally kills Rawana. Rama and Sita are reunited and return to Ayodya.

The final section, "Uttara Kandha," tells how Sita, now pregnant by Rama, is abandoned by him because of his suspicions that she was unfaithful while in Alengka. She is exiled to the forest, and meets the sage Valmiki, who helps raise her twin sons, Kusa and Lava. Eventually, Rama realizes his mistake and goes in search of Sita, but she returns to her mother, the earth. Rama escorts his sons back to the kingdom and passes on the throne to them.

Mahabharata
The story begins with the birth of the blind Dhristarasthra and his younger brother Pandu. Dhristarasthra marries Dewi Gandari and they have 100 sons, collectively called the Korawa. King Pandu has two wives, Dewi Kunti and Dewi Madri, and five sons known as the Pandawa: Yudhistira, Bima, Arjuna, Nakula and Sadewa. After the death of King Pandu, Dhristarasthra becomes the king of Astina. As his successor, he chooses his nephew, Yudhistira. This causes great consternation among his own sons, in particular Duryodhana, who summons all his brothers, friends and allies to destroy Yudhistira and his brothers. They devise all kinds of trickery. Among their strategies is a game of dice, which Yudhistira cannot resist. He gets cheated out of his kingdom. The five brothers, their collective wife Drupadi, and their mother Kunti are exiled to the forest for thirteen years. Many adventures befall them. The climax of the story is the great Bharata Yudha battle between the two family factions.

Bima Swarga
A commonly performed episode from the *Mahabharata*, "Bima Swarga" depicts the convoluted journey of Bima to heaven and hell to free the souls of his father and stepmother. Using his great spiritual powers, Bima transforms his mother and four brothers into parts of his body, enabling them to enter heaven with him. During the journey, Bima witnesses the punishments meted out to those souls who have committed wrong deeds during their lifetime. The climax of the story has Bima successfully releasing the souls of his parents.

Arjuna Wiwaha
Arjuna, one of the five Pandawa brothers, needs to obtain a powerful and *sakti* (magically charged) weapon to fight in the upcoming Bharata Yudha war. He retreats in meditation to the top of Indrakila mountain where he is attacked by various animals and demons in an attempt to disturb his concentration. Undaunted, he completes his meditation. The god Siwa awards him the *keris Pasupati Sastra* and, as wife, the celestial maiden Supraba.

Kunti Sraya
"Kunti Sraya" is an episode from the *Mahabharata* epic which is performed at the daily Barong dances in Batubulan and Singapadu. Kunti (mother of the Pandawa brothers) reluctantly agrees to sacrifice one of her sons to the Goddess Durga. To ensure that

This masked dancer in Kecak, Peliatan, portrays the vehicle of Wisnu in the shape of a bird who tries to save Rama from being killed by a powerful weapon in the form of a serpent.

A Wayang Kulit puppet of Jatayu made by Ida Bagus Belawa from Griya Tebesaya, Peliatan. The Garuda bird can be used either to portray the Jatayu bird in the *Ramayana* or the vehicle of Wisnu.

Kunti keeps her promise, Durga sends her follower Kalika (a demoness) to possess Kunti. Under Kalika's influence, Kunti orders her minister to drag her step-son Sahadewa to the graveyard, where he is tied to a tree. Siwa descends and puts him under a spell of protection. After a failed attempt to kill Sahadewa, Durga realizes that she is defeated and begs Sahadewa to kill her instead. Upon the death of her mistress, Kalika asks for the same punishment but Sahadewa refuses, so she challenges Sahadewa to a fight. He transforms into Barong and she into Rangda. Seeing the Barong in trouble, his followers (village men brandishing *keris*) attack Rangda. Her power is too great and they fall into a fake trance, stabbing themselves until made conscious by sprinklings of holy water.

Panji

These romances, set in twelfth- and thirteenth-century East Java, were composed in the seventeenth and eighteenth centuries. Also known as *Malat*, the stories depict the affairs and interrelationships of four East Javanese kingdoms: Koripan or Jenggala, Daha, Gagelang and Singasari. The central theme is the union of Prince Panji of Koripan with Princess Candrakirana of Daha. They meet and are separated again and again. In many episodes, one in disguise searches for the other.

Babad, the Balinese Chronicles of Kings

The *Babad* are the primary dramatic sources for Topeng mask dance-drama and Wayang Kulit Babad (p. 49). They chronicle the history of Bali's kings and their relationships with other royal families in Java and Lombok. The *Babad* are named after the area described: *Babad Sukawati*, *Babad Gianyar*, *Babad Mengwi* and so on. The most widely sourced is *Babad Dalem*, which tells the history of the major Balinese kings. Some subplots include the arrival of Javanese priests to Bali during the ninth to sixteenth centuries; the founding of major temples and clans; the coronation of kings and the establishment of villages; and the marriages and disputes of some Balinese lineages.

Babad are heroic and didactic in nature. They tell of great battles involving local kings, clan leaders and other heroes. They also convey philosophical concepts, such as the conflicting forces of *dharma* (righteousness, justice, truth) and *adharma* (that which destroys these principles). The performance of a *Babad* story always entails a battle, with *dharma* emerging victorious.

Calonarang, the Story of Black Magic

This eleventh-century East Javanese tale of witchcraft is the basis for one of the most intriguing of Balinese performances (see p. 73).

Four *Calonarang* episodes are commonly used today: "Iyeg Rarung," the dispute between Rarung, one of *Calonarang*'s main disciples and the Minister Madri of Daha; "Katundung Ratna Manggali," Ratna Manggali's rejection by her father, King Erlangga; "Kautus Empu Bahula," the Brahmin Bahula sent as a messenger to Girah to marry Ratna Manggali in order to find out the secrets of the mother; and "Ngeseng Bingin," a competition of magical powers involving a banyan tree.

Tantri, Animal Fables

Tantri Kamandaka, or simply *Tantri*, is a collection of Javanese-Balinese fables about the life of animals, their characteristics and their cunning. Akin to the *1001 Nights*, King Swaryadala is compelled to bed a different virgin every night. Eventually, the only woman left is the beautiful Tantri, daughter of his own minister, Eswaryadala. Rather than succumb, Tantri enthralls the king with a series of animal fables which leads him to revaluate his own actions.

One of the most popular tales in *Tantri* is the story of the wise king Aji Dharma who understands the languages of all animals. A favorite episode tells of a princess who refuses to speak. Whoever can get her to talk shall win her hand in marriage. Aji Dharma and his minister Madrin decide to try their luck. Madrin falls in love with her at first sight. The two men attempt to get her to speak by asking her riddles; Aji Dharma is successful. On the way to Aji Dharma's kingdom, the princess spies some mangoes high up in a tree and implores her husband-to-be to fetch one for her. Leaving his human form, his soul enters the body of a dead monkey. As Aji Dharma scampers up the tree, Madrin seizes the opportunity to project his own soul into Aji Dharma's body and run off with the princess. Aji Dharma then transforms his soul into a parakeet and flies after them. At the kingdom, a number of contests ensue between the "real" and the "fake" Aji Dharma. Two goats, one weak, the other strong, are pitted against each other. Madrin sends his soul into the weak goat in order to strengthen it. While the "fake" Aji Dharma's body is "empty," the real king's soul enters it and, as all stories end, he and the princess live happily ever after.

Jayaprana, the Tragic Tale of Two Lovers

This is the tale of Jayaprana, devoted subject of the king of Kalianget in North Bali, and his sweetheart Layonsari. After they wed, the King of Kalianget becomes infatuated with Layonsari. He sends his minister to take Jayaprana away on false pretenses and kill him. The king goes to Layonsari to convince her to come to the palace with him, but Layonsari grabs his dagger and kills herself. Overcome with grief, the king goes mad, stabs to death members of his court and is, in turn, killed by them.

Rajapala, the First Mixed Marriage

When Rajapala sees the celestial maiden Ken Sulasih and her friends bathing in the river, he falls in love with her and steals her clothes. He will return them only if she agrees to marry him. She relents on the condition that after their first child is born, she will return to heaven. Blessed with a son, Durma, she fulfills her promise and leaves for her celestial home. In his grief, Rajapala goes to meditate in the forest, leaving his son to fend for himself.

Sampik Ingtai, the Chinese "Romeo and Juliet"

This Chinese romance is about two friends, Sampik and Ingtai, who meet at an all-boys school. After many years, Ingtai reveals that he is a woman in disguise, whereupon Sampik falls in love with her. They vow to always be by each other's side as long as they live. At the end of their studies, they go back to their separate homes. Before departing, Ingtai tells Sampik in a riddle that he must not take more than ten days to come and ask for her hand in marriage. She has already been promised to a rich man named Macun, and Sampik arrives too late. Unable to mask his disappointment and embarrassment, he falls sick and dies. Ingtai is distraught. On the way to Macun's house, she asks to pray at Sampit's graveside. The grave opens and she jumps inside to be with him. Another version has the two lovers joyfully reunited.

Ni Wayan Sudiani as Panji in Gambuh, Batuan, 1997. The refined character of Panji (played here by a woman) is about to go to battle against his enemy.

Opposite: A performance of "Kunti Sraya" at Batubulan. Here, Sahadewa leaves his mother Kunti and the prime minister to be sacrificed to the Goddess Durga. The monster Celeluk is in the background.

Wayang Kulit, Shadow Puppet Theater

The oil lamp flickers. A shadow pulsates against the screen. The delicate sounds of the Gender Wayang float through the air. The puppeteer begins his litany, becoming god, clown, princess, demon. The inevitable fight scene ends the story. The Tree of Life makes its last appearance as everyone goes home. Wayang Kulit is an integral part of nearly every temple festival; if the good guys don't always win, at least balance is restored by the end of the play.

Above: The colorful Tree of Life (*kayonan*) as seen from behind the screen. This is one of the most important puppets and appears in the beginning and at the end of the play.

Below: The Tree of Life as seen from the shadow side of the screen. At the conclusion of a *Mahabharata* excerpt, the *kayonan* is placed in the center of the screen while other puppets flank it.

Puppet shows throughout Asia are not only for children, but for people of all ages. In fact, the audience more than likely consists of older males, who savor the philosophical tones of ancient stories. Sleeping children awaken when the music rings loud for the fighting and clown scenes.

Wayang means "shadow" and *kulit* is "leather." These images of cowhide are perforated and painted on both sides. When held up against the cloth screen with an oil lamp behind, the shadows are visible to the audience on the other side. The flickering fire of the coconut oil lamp makes the puppets appear to "breathe" and come to life.

No temple festival is complete without a puppet show. Traditional values are passed on through the stories and the actions of the characters. Philosophical teachings are elucidated through dialog between deities, princes and clowns.

Origins of Wayang Kulit

The art of *pewayangan* (shadow puppetry) originally developed from the animistic belief that every living thing has a soul. Balinese historians claim that Wayang Kulit came from the worship of *pratima* (statues representing the ancestors). This further developed into paintings of the ancestors done on temple walls and then into shadow puppets. The puppets are considered to be the "shadows" of ancestors.

However, no one knows for sure when Wayang Kulit began in Bali. The oldest shadow plays in Asia can be traced to the first century BCE in India. In Indonesia, Wayang only exists in areas where Hinduism reigned, that is, Java, Bali and Lombok.

The first mention of Wayang in Bali is in the *prasasti* (inscription) *Bebetin* dated 896 CE and attributed to King Ugrasena. One hundred and fifty years later, in 1053, the *prasasti Dawan* (Klungkung) describes various artists, including *dalang* (puppeteers). We can therefore assume that Wayang has been performed for over a thousand years.

The Puppet Stage

The screen and its properties all symbolize life on earth. The *dalang* is likened to God, the "great *dalang* in the sky." The *kelir* (screen), stretched across bamboo poles, symbolizes the universe. The *gedebong* (banana tree trunk) at the base of the screen into which the puppets are stuck, is Pertiwi, Mother Earth. The rope used to stretch the screen is symbolic of human muscles and tendons. The *damar* (oil lamp) is the sun, giving life and energy to the world. The lamp is lit with three skeins of thread representing the Hindu gods Brahma, Wisnu and Siwa.

The puppeteer sits in the middle, with the puppets of the "good" side making their entrance from his right, the "bad" side from his left. Puppets not used are propped up on either side of the screen; these represent the pull between left and right. Sitting cross-legged, the *dalang* holds a *cepala* (wooden knocker) between the first and second toes of his right foot. This is used to sound metal clappers hanging from the puppet box or to hit the box itself. A second knocker is often held in the left hand and knocked against the lid on his left. Two assistants untangle and hand him puppets, pour coconut oil into the lamp, and make sure everything goes well. The man on the *dalang*'s left is said to be Wisnu; the one on the right, Brahma.

The Dalang

Probably the most difficult to learn of all Balinese arts is puppetry. A *dalang* not only must be able to re-enact stories in the immense repertoire and know all the characters well, but he must also be able to change vocal qualities instantaneously. The *dalang* is a one-person show; even with assistants and musicians, the play is totally up to the *dalang*. He must manipulate the puppets, chant the numerous classics in the proper metrical form, perform a play appropriate to the situation, lead the musicians, dispense moral advice, and in some cases, act as a priest. And he must hold the audience's attention for hours at a time. Being funny helps.

Book of Rules

No *dalang* dares perform for the first time without thoroughly studying the *Dharma Pewayangan* (Laws of Puppetry). This ancient treatise explains the philosophy of Wayang, instructions on how a *dalang* should conduct himself, mantra (prayer formulas) to protect himself and his puppets, and information on all the ceremonies the *dalang* will officiate over in his function as *mangku dalang* (priest-puppeteer). There are very strict rules of behavior for a puppeteer: dietary restrictions, what direction to face when eating and performing, what foot must go in the door first at the performance venue. If his breath is strongest through the right nostril, his right foot goes over the threshold. The same goes for the left. If it is equal, he jumps!

The puppets are treated as receptacles of living energy, never as playthings. Before the puppet box leaves the house, offerings and prayers are given to the puppets. They are layered in the box in order of sacredness, with animals and demons on the bottom, then weapons, clowns, major characters and the *kayonan* (Tree of Life) at the top. Puppets who have been "killed" in the show must be brought back to life before being put away in the box.

The Meaning of Wayang

The world of illusion is powerful. In Wayang Kulit, the puppets enter and exit the screen. They may engage in battle, they may even be killed. But it is a temporary death. Tomorrow they will appear again in yet another play of life. The world of Wayang is about transience and balance.

A lot of action takes place behind the Wayang Kulit screen. The *dalang* (puppeteer), assisted by his "right and left hand men" and musicians, perform for hours at a time without a break.

Before the show begins, the *dalang* prays to God for guidance. Here, I Wayan Wija concentrates with the *kayonan*.

The puppets represent all the possibilities of human nature. The basic premise of any Wayang show is the struggle for power between good and evil, often represented by rival factions. The Wayang can be seen as an analogy of a person's development: in battle, a young man's resilience is tested. Upon reaching adulthood, there are many temptations to transcend. In order for a person and community to flourish, these demons must be conquered.

The characters of Wayang are there for people to emulate or not. Balinese often refer to someone as being as opportunistic as Sangut, as wise as Bisma, as loyal as Malen or as faithful as Sita. Yet each character has his or her flaws; no one can be perfect.

The Puppets

A *dalang* owns his puppets which number over a hundred. The most important puppet is the *kayonan*, which appears first in the show to symbolize the creation of life as it dances against the screen. This puppet represents the *panca maha bhuta* ("five great elementals" of fire, earth, air, water and ether) which give everything life. It symbolizes the microcosm of the human body and the macrocosm of the cosmos. On screen, it becomes a scene-changer, a tree, fire, sea, clouds, the wind. I Wayan Narta, a puppeteer

from Sukawati, says the word *kayonan* comes from *kayun* ("thought") and that this puppet helps the *dalang* to focus his attention on the performance.

The Punakawan, Clown-Servants

A show could not be held without the four clown-servants, who translate the words of the main characters into colloquial Balinese, keep the pace flowing and provide hours of laughter. There are two puppets for each "side": Twalen (or Malen) and Merdah on the right; Delem and Sangut on the left. These puppets look quite different from the main characters. They are dwarf-like with prominent chins and movable jaws manipulated by a string. Their behavior is crude, burlesque and silly.

Twalen and Merdah are of divine origin. One story recounts that Twalen was formed from the dirt on the body of Sanghyang Tunggal (Supreme God)

and he requested to live among virtuous men. Twalen (Malen) is a fount of knowledge; he has a Third Eye which is inward-looking and shows his wisdom. His son Merdah has a bulbous nose and is constantly looking upwards, giving him a glint of intelligence; he often tries to steer his father towards his own opinion, which is not always the best solution.

The two brothers Delem (Melem) and Sangut are attendants of the antagonists. Delem is a dim-witted cowardly braggart, unable to distinguish right from wrong. He looks like a simpleton with his large round eye and goiter, a sign of spiritual impurity. Sangut is a sly fellow who prefers to be on the side of the "right," while being loyal to the "left." He has a prominent Adam's apple to match his bulging belly. Both of these puppets have tufts of cow hair sticking out from the tops of their heads.

Iconography in the Puppets

Each puppet is tooled with small chisels to make the delicate shadows on the screen. Arms are jointed at the shoulders and elbows. Some demons and clowns have movable legs. A long buffalo horn or wooden rod runs the length of the puppet. The puppeteer holds this or sticks it into the banana tree trunk to keep the puppet in place. The rods enable him to work multiple puppets simultaneously.

Most of the audience sits on the "shadow" side of the screen and cannot see the intricately painted puppets. The audience recognizes the characters by their headdresses and features. The colors assist the *dalang* in remembering which puppet he is manipulating. It can get confusing in the frenzy of battle. Color is not arbitrary, but is associated with particular deities, directions, weapons and numbers.

Characters are divided into *alus* (refined) and *keras/kasar* (coarse), reflected in their coloring, headdresses and costumes. This iconography extends to all dramatic forms. In general, *keras* characters are red or brown. White (Siwa, Bhatara Guru) symbolizes purity, self-control, detachment and is also used for *alus* characters such as Arjuna. Yellow is similar to white but also shows compassion. Green, which symbolizes fertility and steadfastness, is associated with the god Wisnu and his incarnations as Rama and Kresna, who brings prosperity. Black can be used for witches and Twalen. Blue shows bravery and intelli-

gence. Red, associated with Brahma, the creator, and his element fire, brings strife and symbolizes both courage and lack of self-control.

The characters have their own type of crown, bracelets, anklets and clothing which makes them easily identifiable to the audience. Two major types of eyes are *sumpe* (almond-shaped slits) for refined characters and *dedeling* (round) for coarse characters. *Alus* characters either look down or straight ahead as a sign of humility; *keras* characters look up, indicating arrogance and self-importance.

Languages Used

A puppet show begins with an invocation in Kawi (Old Javanese), and most high-status characters speak this language. It is the clowns, in their role as translator-servants, who bring the story into the vernacular. For example, Arjuna speaks in Kawi about a particular task he must do. One of his servants then translates this to his fellow clown in the Balinese language. Most Balinese do not understand Kawi, so this is how the story is transmitted to the audience. The clowns have complete freedom over what they say and do. They bring the world of the past into the present and mock the actions of "high" characters. The audience adores them.

Above and opposite: Wayang Lemah is performed during the day (*lemah* means daytime) as part of the purification rites for rituals. Unlike in regular Wayang Kulit, there is no screen or lamp; a simple line of cotton threads demarcates the boundary between *dalang* and audience. The *dalang* says prayers to the gods (above) before starting his performance.

The *dalang* holds two *cepala* (knockers), one between his toes and the other in his left hand, banging them alternately against the puppet box to emphasize points or to signal a battle.

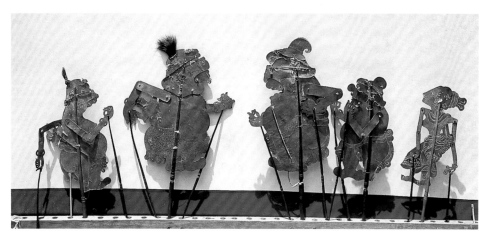

The four *punakawan* or clown-servants and a female maidservant. From left to right: Sangut, Delem, Twalen, Merdah and Condong. These are the translators for the major characters as well as the show-stoppers.

Stories

The majority of Wayang stories are from the *Mahabharata*, especially from the "Bharata Yudha" war between rival cousins of the Pandawa and Korawa factions. Other parts of this great epic are staged, such as "Arjuna Wiwaha" and "Bima Swarga." The *Ramayana* is the second most popular form, and this always involves fight scenes between monkey armies and ogres. Most *dalang* have complete sets of puppets for both epics. Many of the puppets can be used for different characters, for example, Rama and Kresna.

Other Forms of Wayang

Ritual Wayang is usually performed in the morning or late afternoon of a ceremony. At the same time, the *pedanda* (Brahmin high priest) is making holy water. There is no screen. Instead, thick handspun cotton threads are stretched between two branches of the sacred *dapdap* tree about half a meter above the *gedebong*. More than the usual offerings are made before the play begins. Very few people actually watch; it is enjoyed by a more divine audience. The story is always taken from the "Adi Parwa" section of the *Mahabharata*.

Wayang Calonarang is a puppet play about the Queen of Black Magic, Rangda (see pp. 70–5). There are few *dalang* with the skills or desire to perform this as it involves themes of black magic. At one point, the *dalang* will summon all the *leyak* (witches) in the village to challenge him to a magical duel. This is a form of social control as specific local people are named by the *dalang*. The *leyak* puppets are fantastic creations of the imagination: disembodied legs, one-eyed monsters, long flaming-tongued witches.

Wayang Gambuh uses stories from the *Panji* or *Malat* cycle (see pp. 42–3) and is accompanied by

a Gambuh ensemble (see pp. 60–1). The puppets are more elongated and closer in iconography to Javanese puppets. This form was resurrected by the late I Ketut Rindha of Blahbatuh and taught to I Made Sija of Bona and I Wayan Nartha of Sukawati in Gianyar. Nartha still performs it occasionally today.

The late I Ketut Rindha initiated the idea for **Wayang Arja** in 1975 and it was first performed by I Made Sija in 1976. It lost popularity in the 1970s and 1980s. However, Ni Nyoman Candri, a famous Arja dancer and female *dalang*, has recently resurrected this form. The puppeteer uses the singing style of Arja for dialog, accompanied by Gamelan Geguntangan (see pp. 84–5).

New Creations
Wayang Tantri was first performed by I Made Persib at the Indonesian Arts Institute Festival, Bandung, in 1981. In 1983, it was developed and popularized by I Wayan Wija of Sukawati. Using the *Tantri* tales (see p. 43), Wija fashioned a whole new line of animal and human puppets which took Bali by storm. He drew on the music and narratives of Gambuh and incorporated elements of Calonarang into his plots.

The accompaniment consists of a fuller ensemble of drums, gongs and *gender*, called *batel*.

Wayang Babad was created in 1988 for the final examinations at STSI (Indonesian College of the Arts) by I Gusti Ngurah Serama Semadi. Taking the *Babad* (Chronicles of Kings) as its storyline (see p. 42), this new form has yet to find its niche.

Wayang Layar Lebar (large screen shadow puppetry), using electric lights rather than oil lamps, was created by I Ketut Kodi in 1989 at STSI for his final examination. What then became known as **Wayang Listrik** (Electric Wayang) made its debut in 1996 at the Walter Spies Festival and is an out-growth of work done in the United States by filmmaker-puppeteer Larry Reed. Using giant projected shadows on an oversized screen, this form combines puppetry, film, dance, painting and music. Halogen lights are controlled by dimmers which permit instantaneous changes of scene, achieving the effect of filmic cuts and montage. Single point light sources have a continual range of focus so that puppets, backgrounds and actors all appear sharp on the screen. A team of 10–15 shadowcasters are constantly in motion, changing scenery, dancing, moving lights and working puppets

Puppets from the collection of I Wayan Narta, Sukawati. From left to right: Buta Siu, Rangda, Barong, Nang Eblong, Nang Klenceng, Cupak, Rawana.

The puppets Twalen, Bima, Kunti and a priest from the *Mahabharata* story. The major characters are always accompanied by their servants (in this case Twalen, far left) when holding dialogs.

or masks. Reed's work is continued by Sanggar Çudamani in Pengosekan, Ubud.

Wayang Lukluk, or WAKUL, by *dalang* I Rupik has the entire operation on the back of a pick-up truck. When he performs, he simply takes the side panels down and puts up his screen. Known for his humor and outrageous puppets (airplanes, helicopters, motorcycles), purists say this is not real Wayang. But it *is* funny.

Wayang Cengblong is an anachronism for Nang Klenceng and Nang Eblong, the names of two clowns prominently featured in this Wayang Parwa performance. There is much more joking than in a regular Wayang show. This innovation is the brainstorm of *dalang* I Wayan Nardayana CB from Blayu, Tabanan.

Tumpek Wayang

In the Balinese cyclical *wuku* calendar system, a child born during the week of Wayang needs to be given elaborate offerings. Those born on the actual day honoring puppets, Tumpek Wayang, must have a special *wayang sapuleger* performance given at least once in their lives. Otherwise, it is believed that this child could be eaten by the demon-deity Kala. To keep the child from harm, the *dalang* recites the legend of Kala's birth, neutralizing the demon's energy. A special kind of holy water made by the *dalang* is used to purify the child.

Gender Wayang, the Music of the Shadows

The music played to accompany Wayang Kulit Parwa (shadow plays employing stories derived from the *Mahabharata* epic) is Gender Wayang. The basic ensemble has just two pairs of ten-key *gender* (metallophones)—*pemade* (large) and *kantilan* (small)—tuned to the five-note *slendro* scale. The two pairs are an octave apart from one another. As there are no other percussive instruments, the feeling evoked is one of delicate lightness.

If the story is from the *Ramayana* or *Calonarang*, a larger ensemble is used, called Batel Gender Wayang, comprising two *kendang* (drums), *kajar*, *kempur*, *klenang*, *kemong* (all small gongs), and *cengceng* (cymbals). This is also used for Wayang Wong and Parwa dance-dramas.

Gender Wayang can be found everywhere, although playing styles differ. Two of the most popular styles in South Bali are found at Kayumas (Denpasar), popularized by I Wayan Konolan, and in Sukawati (Gianyar) by I Wayan Loceng. Usually only two *gender* are used in North Bali. Unlike the larger ensembles, the musicians or the *dalang* own the instruments.

The *dalang* directs much of the music by giving audio cues, such as hitting the *cepala* against the wooden puppet box to speed things up, and hidden verbal cues, such as having one of the puppets refer to the name of a piece of music.

The musicians sit across from one another, facing their partner. Each player uses two mallets with a wooden disk on the end. The left hand plays the core melody and bass, while the right hand does melodic elaborations and interlocking configurations. Gender Wayang is considered to be the most complex music with elaborate *kotekan* (interlocking configurations) in both odd and even meters which must synchronize with their partner's music. The hands are constantly playing contrapuntally. Damping is done with the outer part of the fourth and fifth fingers, and is quite difficult to do.

Sequencing within the Play

This music begins with the *pamungkah* (opening), conducted while the puppets are taken from their box and placed on the screen; this can last as long as an hour. The *dalang* raps his *cepala* to cue the musicians to play "Alus Harum" (Fragrant Forest), which accompanies the dance of the *kayonan* and invocations of the *dalang*. Throughout the play, *gending* (songs) evoke different moods.

Batel is a simple two-note quick repetition which induces a mood of action for battles. The *angkat-angkatan* (departure) is similar but is a four-note repetition (G#, A, A, A or G#, A, G#, A, for example). There are many moments when the musicians are silent as the *dalang* holds dialogs, the only music being the tapping of the *cepala* for emphasis. The *rebong* (love scenes) consists of three parts: an opening with optional singing by the *dalang*, an interlude, and the final section. The first two sections are slow and soft, the last section, in contrast, loud and a bit burlesque to accompany a parodied scene by one of the clowns and a maidservant. The final piece is "Tabuh Gari." The audience, recognizing the music signaling the end of the performance, all get up to go home.

Other Functions of Gender Wayang

This delicate music is performed for many other functions besides accompanying a shadow puppet performance. For example, at the requisite tooth-filing ceremony, two Gender Wayang musicians play (and women sing sacred *kidung* songs) while the actual filing is taking place. At weddings, two musicians sit on the sidelines and perform throughout the ceremony. At cremations, two musicians flank the cremation tower which carries the corpse to the cemetery. They begin by playing *batel*. At magically dangerous points (such as crossroads), they play "Gending Rundah," a piece which accompanies demons in Wayang Kulit. When approaching the graveyard, they play "Tunjang," associated with Durga, Goddess of Death. When the cremation tower comes to its final resting place in the cemetery, they play "Mesem," a grieving song.

The four Gender Wayang musicians, who play in coodinated pairs, accompany the action on the screen. Note how they hold their mallets.

Dance and Drama: An Introduction

Even though tradition is strong in Bali, change and development in theater and dance are constants. While musicians and dancers continue to weave their respective roles, clowns have broadened their function as social commentators to solo humorists. Television is playing an incredible role in preservation, conservation and distribution of art forms. The modern proscenium stage, with its ability to play with light, is also contributing to change in the arts.

Development of Dance and Drama

For the Balinese, the most popular forms of dance and drama today are the more theatrical genres of Topeng, Arja, Sendratari and Drama Gong, all of which utilize colloquial Balinese, a lot of humor and contemporary themes (even when the story is set in the fifteenth century). Yet these are the very forms that non-Balinese find the most difficult to appreciate because of the language barrier.

With the advent of Kebyar style music and dance in the 1920s, a new form of dance arose called *tari lepas* or pure dance, free of dramatic context. It led to a surge of creativity, continuing into the 1960s. Here the aesthetics of beautiful movement reigned. The relationship of dance to music became much more regimented. Both choreography and music had to be well rehearsed by both dancers and musicians. Solo dances took precedence over dance-dramas. Today, these are the dances that visitors see in commercial venues and the ones Balinese children first learn.

Until the end of the nineteenth century, the arts in Bali had evolved primarily from the courts to the villages or from the religious domain to the secular. Dance-dramas such as Gambuh, Wayang Wong and Topeng were performed in both court and temple settings. Other dance forms, such as Legong, became more prevalent in the nineteenth century but were still very much associated with the courts. By 1908, the Dutch had gained full military and administrative control over Bali. The courts' power and influence receded as well as their role as patrons of the arts. As a result, the wider public had increased freedom to develop and support the arts as they wished.

In the twentieth century, secular art entertainment, with subject matter derived from outside the palace, became much more popular. The Kebyar musical explosion in the early 1900s brought with it a burst of activity in the composition of new works and dances. Women began to take female roles on stage in Arja and Gambuh, reflecting a new status for women in Indonesia. The changing new role for women was partly inspired by Raden Ajeng Kartini, a Javanese princess who called for equal education for females. During this time, while still under colonial rule, Indonesia was already experiencing birth pangs as an emerging nation. In 1928, with the Sumpah Pemuda or Youth Oath of "one nation, one language, one people" the urge towards a nation coalesced. There was much excitement in the air.

Bebancihan or Cross-Dressing

A new form of dance called *bebancihan* or cross-dressing became the rage. There were few refined male roles so these new dances became quite popular among young men. Until the 1920s, women had very few roles on stage. Even the exquisitely feminine Legong was performed by boys up until the 1930s. Men began to perform gentler, more *alus* (refined) dances such as Kebyar Duduk and females were taking on refined male roles such as Panji Semirang and Margapati. In the 1950s,

I Nyoman Nyasih as the fiery-haired monkey Anila in Wayang Wong performed at Yayasan Tejakukus, Tejakula, Buleleng.

Right: Sugriwa, the monkey king from Wayang Wong, in a pose of reverence.

a spate of dances showing everyday life, such as *tenun* (weaving), *nelayan* (fishing) and *tani* (farming), emerged due to the influence of socialism.

While these new *tari lepas* were not considered "sacred dances" per se, they became absorbed in the temple performing circuit. Secular art forms sometimes increase their significance and become associated with religious activities over time. With repeated use in temple repertoire, they become a valid part of ritual. The term "temple dances" does not really apply in Bali. Almost every piece can be performed as part of temple or other ritual activities. However, there are only a few dances—Rejang, Baris Gede, Topeng Pajegan and Mendet—that are actually performed in the sacred, innermost courtyard (*jeroan*) of a temple.

Pragina, the Ultimate Performer

There is no word in Balinese to indicate dancer or actor as such. *Pragina* means both a dancer and an actor as the older forms melded the two together. A performer had to be a virtuoso in dance and drama. In pure dance, the performer expresses the music through facial expressions and body language.

The actors in Drama Gong, while primarily miming everyday movements, also incorporate dance conventions on stage. The word *penari*, which means "dancer" in Indonesian, is often used today to refer to a dancer or an actor-dancer, while the word *pemain/juru* (Indonesian/Balinese) refers to a player or a musician. *Pemain topeng* is a masked performer, while *pemain* or *juru gamelan* is a gamelan musician.

I Ketutu Maria (Mario) performing Kebyar Duduk in the 1920s. Probably the most famous exponent of this dance, performed while seated on the ground, Mario was known for his expressiveness and emotiveness in gesture and body fluidity.

Traditionally, each village had its own performing troupe or would ask a neighboring village to provide entertainment for a temple ceremony. Certain villages became famous for a particular genre of dance or drama: Batuan for Gambuh, Singapadu for Arja, Peliatan for Legong, Jagaraga for Kebyar creations, Negara for Jegog, Kedaton for Janger, and so forth. These troupes are called *sebuna*, meaning that their performers all come from one village or *banjar*.

The All-Star Troupe

In the late 1960s, however, a new phenomenon occurred, that of the all-star troupe. The sponsors of the event, for example the village temple committee or a family celebrating a wedding, can pick and choose an all-star cast of dancers and actors (but not musicians) to perform together. For a Topeng masked dance, this usually consists of five dancer-actors. The roles of the Panasar, clown-servant storytellers, are a pair of actors used to working together, an Abbott and Castello kind of team. The other three actors might come from different villages and may not have performed together before. The actors decide on several things before the performance begins. First, the story, which depends on the context: a tale of a royal marriage from the past might be the choice for a wedding. A re-enactment of the Eka Dasa Rudra ritual at Besakih might be performed at a large temple ceremony. Secondly, they discuss who will act which roles. With possible exceptions of set comic pieces by the clowns, the entire performance is improvised, showing the consummate skill of the Balinese actor.

I Nyoman Regug as one of the Panasar (clown-servant storytellers) in Barong. The Panasar plays a very important role in dramatic forms as it is he who keeps the story going.

53

In the Barong dance-drama, oftentimes men in the audience go into trance, taking a *keris* (dagger) and stabbing first Rangda the witch, and when that fails, turning the *keris* on themselves. These men are followers of the Barong (white, protective magic) and wish to destroy Rangda (dark, black magic). Here, a priest sprinkles a man with holy water to bring him out of trance.

Structure in Classical Drama

In the more classical forms, there is a set structure for each character. The performer first hesitates to come out from behind the curtain (*langse*), shaking it and taking a long time in opening it. If no curtain is used, the character might emerge from the *kori agung* (temple or palace gates). This is akin to warming up the audience for each character and allows time for the *pragina* (performer) to get used to his or her role. This is called *ngugal*, or the introductory dance. The servants always precede their master or mistress, literally setting the stage for their entrance. With the advent of Kebyar forms, this elaborate introduction has been replaced by a short, quick miming of the curtain opening (*mungkah lawang*), allowing no time for either dancer or audience to adjust to the character.

The Concept of Duality

Almost every Balinese dance form incorporates elements of *alus* (refinement) and *keras* (coarseness); of male and female movements; of more static positions called *agem* and transitory movements called *angsel*. Dances usually begin with a gradual build-up in the tempo and then taper off again. Within a dance, there are *alus* and *keras* movements; the body and the arms move up and down; there is stillness and great spurts of movement. This play between opposites can be seen in all Balinese arts and in many aspects of the religion.

Role of the Clowns

One of the many beauties of Balinese dance-dramas is the way they bridge two worlds: the past and the present. The stories are mostly set in the distant past, and presented in a narrative form. The archaic language used is Kawi, which the audience usually does not understand. The Panasar's (clown-servants) role is to make the past accessible by interpreting messages from the ancestors and transmitting them to the contemporary audience. Otherwise, drama would be a static form with only "historical significance," such as Gambuh. The clowns also serve as a means to provoke self-scrutiny on the part of the audience. Through humor, they comment on the absurdities and oddities of the "outside world." Language also has an important role. Plays on words and interplay between various languages (Indonesian, Balinese, English and Japanese) provide for a rich verbal texture.

In the 1960s, with the advent of Sendratari and Drama Gong, the role of the Panasar was replaced with the sole storyteller or *dalang* in Sendratari. The servants in Drama Gong have become clowns only, rather than interpreters as they are in the Topeng and Arja. The text or narrative has lost its importance in these more modern forms.

Interaction of Dance and Music

Music is not just an accompaniment for Balinese dance; it is the energy of the dance. Music creates moods and provides accentuations (*angsel*) and frames for movement sequences and phrases. This means that the dancer must understand the music.

There are two means of interaction between dancers and musicians. First, the dancer follows the musical structure of the accompaniment. The length and dynamics are dictated by the music and cannot be changed or improvised during the performance. Thus the dancer's freedom is restricted. All Kebyar dances fall into this category. In the second option, the musical changes are dictated by the dance and musicians follow the dancer's cues. The dancer has improvisational freedom within the basic choreographic concept. In Jauk, Topeng Arja, Baris and Barong, the dancer can arrange movements spontaneously on stage. There is a codified movement vocabulary but the order of presentation is left to the dancer. The skill of the dancer and the ability to sense audience reaction determines the length of the piece. The stronger the rapport with the musicians, the more inspired the dancer becomes. For the clowns, improvisation rules and the musicians take their cues from the clowns.

In popular dance-dramas, the *pragina* give signals to the gamelan to speed up or to stop. When they want to be heard, the clowns clap their hands once, and at the end of the gong cycle the gamelan stops playing. There is usually enough time for the musicians to smoke or drink coffee while waiting for their cue to begin again. If the clowns are funny, it could be a good 20 minutes.

The drummers and the *ugal* (lead metallophone) player watch the dancer carefully for cues as to when to change the dynamics or the speed of the music. In Jauk, the drummer uses his hands on the drum and the dancer his feet, teasing each other to produce similar rhythms.

The dancer becomes a musician in Kebyar Trompong, Palawakia, Janger, Cakepung, Genjek, Kecak and dance-dramas where singing is an integral part of the form, such as Arja, Topeng and Gambuh. In Wayang Kulit, the *dalang* controls all the musical cues. By beating his puppet box with the *cepala* (wooden knob) held between his toes or by verbal cues, the musicians will know when to change tempo or what songs to play.

Sometimes famous dancers bring their drummers with them to lead local gamelan groups. But when dancers are invited to perform at a village festival, it is usually only the dancers who come. They are accompanied by the local gamelan group, with whom they probably have never performed in the past. There is no prior rehearsal. This type of "impromptu harmonizing" is one of the unique features of Balinese performing arts.

Interaction with the Audience

One of the delights of Balinese dance and drama is that the audience is right there with the performers. The *pragina* are in constant eye contact with their audience and can easily gauge how their performance is measuring up (or not). When the clowns hit the funny bone, they continue hitting. If not, then they signal the gamelan to play the "exit" song. In some forms, such as Gambuh, the "green room" is next to the gamelan and consists of a woven mat where the dancers sit and wait for their next entrance. They may even chat with the musicians or audience. Animals are also a part of the festivities. Dogs frequently take center stage for a few moments until they are chased off. And of course, the children will scream and run around the instruments and the stage space before showtime and sometimes even during it. If it rains, then the performance comes to a hasty end.

Props and Lighting

There are few stage props in Balinese theater. For the traditional stage or *kalangan*, there is only a split curtain (*langse*) hung at one end of the performing area. The gamelan musicians face each other perpendicular to the *langse*, and often the drummers, *kajar* (time-keeper) and *ceng-ceng* (cymbals) players sit near the curtain. The audience sits wherever there is space, even in a musician's lap for young children. Chairs

are a new element and are usually only provided for certain kinds of entertainment where the performers are on an elevated stage space, such as at a *bale banjar* (community hall).

Lighting of any kind is minimal. Before the advent of electricity in the mid-1970s, kerosene and pressure lamps were hung at strategic points of the *kalangan*. Now, cheaper fluorescent bulbs are hung along with microphones placed at three or four points above the stage floor. The placing of microphones, along with the introduction of television, has changed the staging quite a bit as now the actors must be certain they end up under a microphone so they can be heard. Televised performances are set up like a proscenium stage; consequently, many of the conventions of the traditional "in-the-round" *kalangan* stage are lost. Actors project to the camera instead of to one another.

Kreasi baru **or new creations are all the rage today and consist primarily of large dance-dramas based on Sendratari styles. This is a fighting scene from Nara Kusuma Sendratari, performed at the Ardha Chandra Ampitheater during the Bali Arts Festival, 2004.**

Sacred and Ceremonial Dances

There are several dances which are considered more sacred than others: Rejang, Pasutri, Mendet, Baris Gede and Topeng Pajegan. These are usually performed in the innermost courtyard (*jeroan*) of the temple. Part of what makes them more "sacred" is that there is little or no rehearsal of the forms; they are performed for the deities and it is not the compactness of the form that takes precedence in the ritual, but the actual presence of the form.

Rejang

There are many different types of Rejang, a group dance done by prepubescent girls, unmarried females or post-menopausal women, depending on the village. They are said to be the *bidadari* (heavenly maidens) come to earth. The girls or women face the shrines of their deities and dance towards them with simple foot movements, their arms outstretched to the side. In some versions, they form a circle and hold the waist scarf of the dancer in front of them. In 1988, Ni Luh Swasthi Wijaya Bandem of STSI choreographed a new version that combined movements of many types of Rejang. Called Rejang Dewa, this dance has now become the standard in many villages throughout the island and is recognized for its tall crowns made of coconut palm fronds decorated with marigold flowers.

The regency of Karangasem is famous for its different kinds of Rejang: the village of Asak performs Pendet Rejang every Kuningan holiday and for Ngusabha Kasa (a temple festival which falls in June/July every year). The costumes are unique; the young women wear semicircular headdresses of gold *sasak* flowers with round, circular white disks framing the face. The dance itself is quite simple with two lines of dancers who present special *prani* offerings to a group of 24 older women called Jro Krama Saing. This dance precedes the main ritual of the temple. This is one of the few places in this area which has a Gamelan Gong Kebyar accompanying the dance.

In the neighboring village of Bungaya, the headdresses (*onggar-onggar*) are even more spectacular. They look like a mountain of filigreed gold with one long branch sticking out of the center. The *daha* (young, unmarried women) are wrapped in a special red *kerah* cloth which leaves their shoulders bare. The movements for this Rejang are also simple, with a basic up and down lifting of the arms. The Gamelan Selonding accompanies this and other dances done in this area of East Bali.

In Tenganan Pegeringsingan, Bali's most famous Bali Aga (aboriginal Balinese) village, Rejang is performed in January/February and June/July during celebrations. Young women usually dress in the unique *geringsing* (double ikat) cloths. The dance consists of simple movements. Abuang is another dance done here, where young men and women greet one another using restrained gestures.

In Gianyar, a form of Rejang is done by a mixture of older and younger women called *sutri* at temple festivals. In the village of Batuan, the Rejang is called Pasutri. Every night for nearly six months, 25–100 females, from toddlers to great-grandmothers, gather at the large pavilion outside the Pura Desa temple. In lines at the western end of the hall, they very slowly proceed to the piles of offerings at the eastern end. It takes nearly half an hour to advance 20 meters. The slow movements and constant shifts of weight give the illusion of a sea of women undulating back and forth.

Aside from its beauty, this is a dance of exorcism.

In the Samuan Tiga temple of Bedulu, older women called *permas* dance Rejang to help purify the temple area.

In Bungaya, East Bali, elaborate headdresses (*onggar-onggar*) and simple movements make up the Rejang dance.

acter has its own movement vocabulary. The role is further defined by the headdress and costume worn.

Every play begins with the entrance of the Condong (maidservant), who is a strong female character. Her voice is alto and her movements are large and staccato. The servant always precedes the royal character, describing the beauty of her mistress. After her solo, the *kakan-kakan* or ladies-in-waiting (4–8 young women) enter to dance with the Condong. Their movements are more *alus*. Then the quintessence of refinement arrives: the Princess. Wearing a long train, she kicks it elegantly out of her way as she moves. Her movements are subtle and slow and her voice is a high soprano. She only speaks in refined Middle Javanese language while her maidservant translates into Balinese. The high characters hold court, give speeches, and engage in dialog with their underlings.

Sequence of the Play

The remaining order of the play depends on the story being used. Following is a typical Panji-centered tale.

In the second act, the *arya* (strong knights) of Prince Panji enter and speak while dancing. Rangga, an *alus* aide to Panji (his costume is quite similar), enters and dances with the *arya*. Panji then appears, taking small, mincing steps and speaking in a near falsetto. It is only now that the story is revealed.

The third act brings out the antagonists. First to enter are Demang and Tumenggung, the servants of the strong king (Prabu Keras). They wear elaborate make-up and have distinctive headdresses. If there is any humor expressed in this form, these two will be the ones to do it. Then Rangga meets with Prabu Keras, who enters with his servant Togog.

The fourth act belongs to the refined king or Prabu Manis who enters with his servant Turas. A dialog ensues. The fifth act revolves around Prabangsa, strong king and adversary of Panji. He enters with his servant and Potet, a young boy. The last act is a battle between Panji and his foot soldiers and Prabangsa with his men.

When watching Gambuh, it is best not to try and follow the story but rather to appreciate the beauty of the movements and costumes, the cadence of the gamelan and the ambience evoked.

The center for this classical form is the village of Batuan in Gianyar regency. The Ford Foundation funded the resurrection and preservation of Gambuh here so successfully that now Gambuh is performed at the Pura Desa in Batuan on the first and fifteenth day of every month. At nearly every *odalan* in Batuan, a version of Gambuh is done. Other places where it is occasionally performed are Pedungan and Tumbak Bayuh (Badung), Padang Aji and Budakeling (Karangasem), and Depehe, Naga Sepaha and Anturan (Buleleng). Remants of this form can be found in Apit Yeh and Baturiti in Tabanan and on Nusa Penida island.

Ni Made Sarniani in the role of the Putri or Princess, at Besakih. The princess must be played by a tall and slender woman. In contrast, her maidservant, the Condong, is short and has a fuller figure. The Princess's long train is flipped out of her way as she saunters around the stage space.

Wayang Wong, Masked Ramayana

The dramatic form of Wayang Wong is rarely performed today, so if you get a chance to see this ancient masked form, do so. The Balinese consider Wayang Wong and its masks sacred. The masks, kept in the temple, are taken out and blessed during festivals but not necessarily danced. *Wayang* means "shadow" and often refers to the ancestors; *wong* means "human." Using the conventions of Wayang Kulit (shadow puppetry), the dancers move in a stylized fashion. The stories told are from the epic *Ramayana* and many of the characters are monkeys.

Twalen is a servant to King Rama, but his role is much greater than that. He is considered to be half-god half-man and is the consummate advisor.

Laksman, Wibisana and the monkey army prepare themselves for battle in a Wayang Wong performance at Mas.

History

The King of Klungkung, Dalem Gede Kusamba (1772–1825), asked his dancers to create a new form of dance-drama using the *Ramayana* story for its plot and a collection of royal masks. Headdresses and costumes were made according to the iconography used in Wayang Kulit, and the new form was called Wayang Wong.

The dancers imitate the gestures of shadow puppets. Unlike Wayang Kulit, where the story is paramount, here the movements take precedence. Most of the scenes include fighting, with Rama and his army winning in the end. The actors sing their lines and long, drawn-out dialogs are held in Kawi. In most villages, a single episode is performed at one time.

Waning in popularity over the centuries, Wayang Wong can now be found in fewer than twenty villages in Bali. The most active troupes today are in Tejakula (Buleleng), Pujung Kaja, Dentiis and Mas (Gianyar), Kamasan and Nusa Penida (Klungkung), Apuan and Suluhan (Bangli), Tunjuk (Tabanan), Wates Tengah (Karangasem) and Bualu (Badung).

The Storyline

Taking its storyline from the *Ramayana*, the theme of the play is essentially about good and that which destroys it. This dance-drama is easy to follow (see pp. 40–2). The evil ogre king of Alengka, Rawana, abducts Sita, wife of King Rama. The heroic bird Jatayu tries to rescue her but is killed by Rawana and consequently found by King Rama and his brother Laksmana. Hanuman, the Monkey Commander, then offers to assist with his vast army of monkeys. In the end, Sita is reunited with her husband.

Victory over Demons

Many Balinese rituals revolve around the neutralization of spirits of chaos and Wayang Wong is often done at Galungan and Kuningan, holy days which celebrate the victory of *dharma* (truth) over *adharma* (injustice). In fact, in Tejakula, the performance is credited with helping to stave off pest attacks on citrus trees that grow in abundance there.

Music

Wayang Wong is accompanied by a small-sized ensemble known as Batel Gender Wayang (see pp. 50–1). The music is repetitive in nature and fast in tempo as most of the scenes involve fighting. In this ensemble, the *gender* metallophones become the melodic leader. There are specific melodies for meetings, romance, sorrow and battles. The melodies used here are more or less the same as those used in the shadow puppet play Wayang Kulit Ramayana.

Characters and Masks

Wayang Wong masks differ from those found in Topeng. Carved out of wood, they are decorated with ear ornaments (*rumbing*) and leather side pieces (*sekar taji*), attached to tooled leather headdresses. All the monkey characters have tails which curve up and out from the waist. Except in Tejakula and Pujung Kaja, the refined roles (Rama, Sita, Laksmana and Wibisana) are unmasked.

Some of the main characters are:

Rama: The wise king par excellence, the ultimate in *alus* (refinement).

Laksmana: Rama's younger brother.

Malen (or **Twalen**): The son of Siwa, a demigod and a wise advisor to his Lord Rama. He is one of the most beloved characters. In many villages this mask is highly revered and has special magical properties. He wears a dusty dark *saput* (cape) with a bamboo hoop skirt or thick padding underneath to give him the appearance of a heavily set man.

Merdah: Translator for Rama and assistant to his father, Malen. He trots along with youthful glee. An enthusiastic learner, he respectfully listens to what Malen has to say. His red mask sports a bulbous nose.

Delem: Servant to Rawana. He thinks he knows everything and struts around with his nose in the air. Bulging eyes show his demonic nature.

Sangut: Delem's younger brother, the quintessential pure-of-heart fool. He dearly loves his brother, but would prefer to be on the side of the good guys. His mouth droops and his eyes protrude.

Rawana: The demon king from Alengka, who desires everything. His cruel mouth shows his greediness, while his bulging eyes and fangs prove his demonic nature.

Indrajit (also known as **Meganada**): Rawana's son, very much like his father.

Wibisana: Rawana's younger brother, but his true nature is on Rama's just side.

Kumbakarna: Another of Rawana's brothers, a giant in the extreme. His love of food and sleep sometimes gets the better of him. His mask is considered to be magically powerful in many villages.

Hanuman: The white Monkey Commander, who can fly as he is son of Bayu, God of the Wind. Totally selfless, his courage is unmatched and his loyalty to Lord Rama without compare.

Sugriwa and **Subali**: Twin monkey brothers, they fight over the celestial maiden Dewi Tara. Their masks and costumes are the same; in some villages the only difference is in the color of the sash.

Jatayu (often called **Garuda**): The king of birds, who dies trying to rescue Sita for Rama.

Hanuman

King Rama

Twalen and Merdah

Laksmana

Jatayu

Topeng, Masked Dance-Drama

There are many masked dance-dramas in Bali, but Topeng is the richest in its variety of masks and movements. Popular among the Balinese for the stories of their own ancestors, this form is an important part of rituals. The play begins with a series of solo dances of ministers who set the stage for the royal characters to come. A problem needs to be resolved and the villagers (played by hysterical clowns) come to assist. In the end, the good king wins.

Top to bottom: The masks of Topeng Dalem (the refined king), Topeng Keras (a strong prime minister) and Topeng Tua (an elderly man).

Right: The elegant gestures of the refined king, Topeng Dalem, as he instructs his people, exemplify his royal heritage. His headdress, bedecked with frangipani flowers, quivers gracefully as he walks.

The Roots of Topeng

Topeng is one of the most popular forms of dance-drama. *Topeng* literally means "to close or press against the face," and the dancer always wears a mask. The stories used in Topeng chronicle the lives of Balinese kings (and occasionally a queen) rather than the Indian *Ramayana* and *Mahabharata* epics. One reason the Balinese enjoy Topeng so much is that it tells the history of their own people through movement, song, and dialog/monologue.

In the *Prasasti Bebetin* (*prasasti* is an ancient text, usually inscribed on small metal sheets) dating back to the Caka year 818 (896 CE) is found the word *petapukan* (*tapuk* means "to cover" or mask). It may be assumed that Topeng existed at this time. Until the twentieth century, the most popular form of Topeng was Topeng Pajegan, a masked dance performed by one actor. The first masks had mouth pieces (*canggem*) that the dancer bit on to hold the mask in place. Today, masks in Bali are held on by a rubber strap.

Characters

Topeng is done for *odalan* (temple festivals) and a myriad of other rituals. In a traditional performance, five men play all the roles (called Topeng Panca, meaning "five dancers") simply by changing masks and headdresses. The drama begins with the *panglembar* or introductory characters who pave the way for the entrance of the king. The dancer shows off his virtuosity through pure dance movements. The three most popular masks are Topeng Keras, a strong prime minister character with a red or brown face denoting strength and courage; Topeng Keras Bues, strong yet goofy with bulbous eyes and large, humorous movements; and the beloved Topeng Tua, an old man who remembers his youth. He stumbles, wipes the sweat off his brow, breathes heavily with exertion and blows his nose. These characters do not speak, but move around the stage space, the prime ministers sweeping it of any enemies before their Lord appears on stage.

The Dalem (king) is the quintessence of refinement. Moving with small, mincing steps, his body curves through space rather than cutting brashly through it. His white mask has mother-of-pearl teeth and a prominent gold ornament between his eyes. He never speaks, but only gestures, allowing his servants to do his talking for him.

Panasar, the Clown-Servants

The next characters to appear are the storytellers (*panasar*), roles of two brothers who wear half-masks enabling them to speak. They are like the bards in Shakespearian plays. The older brother (Panasar Kelihan) begins by singing his tale behind the dance curtain. Stepping into the stage arena, he regales the audience with glorious facts about his Lord and his kingdom. Only then does he drop hints about which king, what century and which place he is talking about. He then calls for his younger brother (Panasar Cenikan) Ketut, whom he always accuses of being invariably late and lazy, despite the fact that it is this brother who philosophizes and educates the audience.

These two traverse around the stage space discussing the issues of the day, always with humor that leaves the audience chortling. It is their responsibility to keep the storyline going as well as integrate modern references into the ancient stories (such as too much development or the annoyance of so many handphones ringing while they are trying to tell the story). Thus the audience can appreciate both worlds at the same time. In this way, the actor-dancers impart important religious and moral issues without sounding too pedantic.

Advice is better relayed through anecdote than lecture and Topeng dancers are adept at this type of edification.

The two Panasar bring up the problem or issue at hand: a princess has been kidnapped, land has been stolen, a large ceremony is to be held. Then the music suddenly changes and the two go into supplicating postures, sitting on the floor cross-legged with their hands set in respective poses. The Dalem then appears between the two halves of the curtain, his flowered headdress quivering. His movements are dainty and refined and his mask a light cream color with mother-of-pearl teeth shining below his trimmed moustache. He sits on the top of a chairback to show his status. He then approaches his servants and tells them through gestures what needs to be done. One Panasar speaks for the king as it is difficult to speak through a full mask, and also unseemly for such a refined character, and the other simultaneously translates into colloquial Balinese for the audience. The king then exits.

Bondres, the Clowns

The brothers decide to gather their friends and allies together, whether an army or their neighbors in the *banjar* (hamlet). Here the clowns (*bondres*) come in, with multiple layers of teeth, stutters, gimpy legs, deaf ears and monkey faces. They are said to represent the masses, the opposite spectrum of royalty. Sleeping children in the audience wake up now. The actor who plays Panasar

Kelihan stays on stage while his younger brother goes backstage, changes and re-enters with one of the other actors who also played an introductory role. These two are clowns now, wearing different masks and headgear. The brilliance of Balinese improvisation really shines here as the actors banter back and forth on issues of the day, contemporizing events that happened hundreds of years ago and making fun of everybody, from priests to cab drivers to tourists!

If the plot involves an enemy, perhaps a kidnapper or land snatcher, the villains make their entrance before the clowns. The evil king has bulging eyes and a red or brown visage showing his coarseness, in contrast to Dalem, the refined king.

Topeng Pajegan, the Ritual

Another type of masked dance is called Topeng Pajegan in which one actor performs all the characters alone. This is only performed for rituals, such as temple festivals, usually in the inner courtyard as the *pedanda* (Brahmin high priest) prepares holy water for the ritual. The main difference between Topeng Pajegan and Topeng Panca, aside from the number of dancers, is the last mask. In Topeng Pajegan, the last character to emerge is Sidhakarya, with an offering in his hands. Sidhakarya, which means "to finish the task," refers to the ceremony at hand. Wearing a white mask with narrow slits for eyes, buck teeth, and sporting wild white hair, he is indeed frightening. With sparse movements he hops around and laughs eerily. Carrying an offering bowl, he throws yellow rice to the four directions, dispensing wealth and fertility to everyone. He snatches up a young child from the audience, and gives him or her Chinese coins with square holes in the center, a symbol of prosperity.

I Ketut Kantor and I Ketut Wirtawan recount that in the time of King Dalem Waturenggong of Gelgel (1551–1651), a large ceremony called *nanglukmerana* was held at Besakih temple to eradicate the island of pestilence. At the time of preparation for this grand ritual, a Brahmin named Ida Brahmana Walasakia came from Keling, Java, with the purpose of assisting the king. Because of his rough and menacing appearance, the king had him ousted. This did not please the Brahmin and he cursed the kingdom with drought and illness; the ritual did not even take place. The king regretted his actions and looked far and wide for

Above: Topeng Tua tentatively opens the curtain, taking his time to stand up and dance.

Below: With bold and energetic gestures, the strong prime minister, Topeng Keras, is not afraid to show his stuff.

Walasakia, whom he eventually found, asked his forgiveness and was absolved. The island returned to normal and Walasakia was given the title Dalem Sidhakarya as he was able to restore prosperity. It is said that a mask was then made in the image of Walasakia: a bit frightening, rowdy and powerful. This mask is Topeng Sidhakarya.

A Topeng Pajegan dancer must be more than just a performer. He undergoes a special purification ceremony (*mewinten*). He must be able to perform all the characters in a Topeng play, know the *Babad* (historical chronicles) and be fluent in both Balinese and Kawi. Songs must be memorized, and storytelling technique perfected. Above all, his knowledge of religion and philosophy must be profound.

Today, one might see a performance of Topeng Sidhakarya by two or three dancers. This is because it is becoming more difficult to find one person able to dance all the different parts as well as fulfill the ritual obligations that a Sidhakarya mask demands.

Topeng Prembon and Topeng Sakti, Recent Developments

The 1940s saw the rise of Prembon, which means "mixed" because it has masked as well as unmasked roles from the Arja operetta form. These unmasked characters, usually played by women, alternate their singing with spoken lines. This is extremely popular with the Balinese. The most recent development is Topeng Sakti, an all-women's group, which performed at the 2001 Magdelena Festival in Denmark. The musicians were women from the Mekar Ayu gamelan group in Pengosekan, Ubud, and the dancers were Ni Nyoman Candri and Cokorda Isteri Agung from Singapadu and Cristina Formaggia from Italy.

Backstage

A Topeng story may be chosen in several ways. The host might request a particular episode, or the actors might choose one based on current local issues. They also take into account their own respective skills. The story must include an audience scene with the king, and the appearance of the villagers, and must conclude with a fight or meeting scene. This is the aesthetic structure of a Topeng performance.

Balinese dramatic forms differ greatly from Western forms in how the scripting is determined. In a Topeng with five actors, a troupe which consistently performs together has certain routines already worked out. It is also possible that the host, whether a temple committee or a family holding a ceremony, may invite certain, specific dancers. These dancers may never have performed together prior to this event. The host arranges transportation and dinner for the performers, who then ask what story the host requires. For a wedding, the host may request the story of a famous king's marriage. At a temple ceremony, a story about a grand and wondrous ritual held long ago may be appropriate. If the host has no preference, the actors ask what has been happening lately in the village. Perhaps the village head has had his hand too deep in the coffers. Then, the dancers choose the story of a long ago greedy king. The audience, including the long-handed one, gets the message. The actor-dancers do not have much time to work out their lines. Nor do they rehearse with each other or the gamelan orchestra. Usually this impromptu group has never been accompanied by the local musicians before. Thus, a group of dancer/actors who have never yet performed together, joins with a group of musicians they have not worked with before, and in a matter of minutes, they agree upon a story, plot, musical accompaniment and perform straightaway with no rehearsal, in a play that lasts 3–4 hours—proof again of the extraordinary improvisational skills of Balinese performers.

Each dancer brings along a box of masks, various headdresses, and their own costumes. Before starting, a small ritual is conducted by one of the dancers to ensure the success of the performance. The masks and headdresses are set in a high place of respect, never touching the ground, and incense is wafted towards them. The dancers shake the curtain, signaling the gamelan and the show begins.

Making a Balinese Mask

Ida Bagus Anom of Mas and Ida Bagus Alit of Lod Tunduh shared how they make a Balinese dance mask. First, on an auspicious day, the carver must go to the graveyard where the *pule* (*Alstonia scholaris*) tree grows. This wonderfully light wood (between balsam and pine) is the perfect medium for a mask. Offerings are made and permission requested to take wood from the trunk of the tree. The mask-maker then chops a rough shape in the wood with a hand axe. He waits for inspiration as to which mask to make. Using a set of different sized chisels, he begins to shape it. Once the form is finished, he uses curved knives and sandpaper to smooth it. Painting the mask is a long, tedious process. Traditional pigments are made

A Topeng Story

On the island of Nusa Penida, southeast of Bali, lived the cruel and ruthless king Dalem Bungkut. Some of his oppressed subjects went to Gelgel to request help from the king who sent his minister, Gusti Jelantik Putra, to kill Dalem Bungkut. But Dalem Bungkut's magic was too strong and he could not be defeated.

When Gusti Jelantik Putra and his wife Ayu Keniten were bathing in the river, a small piece of *dadap* wood repeatedly bumped her stomach. Each time she pushed it away. They took it home and just as they were about to throw it on the kitchen fire, a voice spoke out, "I am a tusk of the Naga Basuki and the King of Nusa will die through me alone," and a *keris* (dagger) appeared inside the wood.

When Gusti Jelantik Putra left for Nusa Penida, his wife insisted upon coming along. She brought the magic *keris*. They were treated with great hospitality, but Gusti Jelantik Putra was ridiculed by Bungkut, certain that no weapon could harm him. Angered, Putra rushed the king with his *keris*, but the blows glanced off of him. Then Ayu Keniten gave her husband the powerful dagger. Seeing the *keris*, Bungkut shook with fear and knew his time had come. He bequeathed all his land and wealth to the King of Gelgel and died.

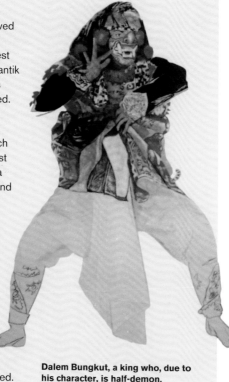

Dalem Bungkut, a king who, due to his character, is half-demon.

Opposite: I Wayan Dibia as Sidhakarya. The last mask of a Topeng Pajegan ritual is the Sidhakarya, symbolizing that the sacred work is finished.

Mask-maker I Wayan Tangguh of Singapadu ponders his work, that of a *naga* serpent mask.

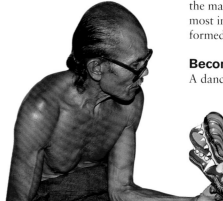

from stones and fish or pig bones ground and mixed with boiled fish or cow skin glue. Up to forty layers of color are applied, and the mask is dried in the sun between each application. The finishing touches are the mustache, hair and eyebrows made of goat hair. A number of ceremonies must be performed for masks used in sacred dances (see pp. 16–17). Since the mask-maker has held the wood with his feet, the most impure part of the body, a ritual must be performed to cleanse the mask.

Becoming One with the Mask

A dancer, in order to become one with the mask so that he can bring it to life on stage, will often hold it in his hand and look at it—trying to discern the power that it holds within. A mask dancer will often sleep with a new mask on the wall facing him so that the essence of the mask enters him as he sleeps.

The Story of Durga Uma Dewi

Why is *pule* wood used for making masks? The story is fascinating. According to Ida Bagus Alit of Lod Tunduh, the god Bhatara Siwa, feeling a bit frisky, desires his wife Bhatari Giri. Inconveniently, he had cursed and banished her to earth to live out her days. In demonic form as Bhatari Durga, she was not permitted to return to heaven and remained in the graveyard. Desiring her, Bhatara Siwa promises a meeting at midnight in the cemetery, but he is a little late. Bhatari Giri had taken some pains with her appearance and was infuriated by the delay. She transformed herself into Durga Murti, a demoness satisfied only with human flesh, sporting a horrific demon head complete with long sharp fangs. Simultaneously, she appeared as the beautiful Durga Uma Dewi, the positive aspect of Bhatara Siwa.

When Bhatara Siwa arrives and sees his wife in the demonic form, he knows he is in trouble. Inside the Pura Dalem (Temple of the Dead), he transforms himself into Rudra Murti, the half-animal half-human being known as the Barong. To fight Rangda, he must be like her. They meet. Rangda plays hard to get. In Bhatara Siwa's excitement, he ejaculates, but his sperm alone cannot become human. Instead, it becomes *eka pramana* (one element/one power), taking the form of a tree. *Dwi* (two) *pramana* are the animals who act instinctively towards survival, but are incapable of reflection. Humans, however are *tri pramana*, having the three powers of action, word and thought—*bayu*, *sabda*, *idep* (see p. 11).

The story goes that from the ejaculated sperm grew the *pule* tree (from the words *pul*, meaning "strong desire," and *lipia*, meaning "forgetting oneself"). This is the wood used to make the sacred masks of Rangda and Barong as well as other dance masks. A saying in Balinese, related to the nature of the *pule* wood, is "Pekidihang ada, anggon tusing ada," meaning that "you give advice to other people but you don't take that advice for yourself." When one cuts a slice of wood from a *pule* tree to make a mask, the bark never grows back, signifying that it never heals. This is a metaphor for someone who considers himself wise, yet still has his own issues which need to be resolved. The bark of the *pule* tree is used in traditional Balinese medicine for fevers and other illnesses; the tree itself is highly revered.

Barong, Rangda and Dancers of Dharma

The playful lion-like Barong and the menacing witch Rangda are two sides of a coin. Both village protectors, their power comes to the fore in dramas depicting their escapades. All the stories involving these two characters are steeped in black magic and invariably induce trance in either the performers or the audience. There are many forms of the Barong, the most common being a four-legged furry creature sporting a spectacular costume.

A Telek dancer in Jimbaran rests in between acts. The tall headdress is made out of gilded leather. The white mask denotes purity, as the Telek are representatives of the good side.

The Tiger Barong is not as common as the Barong Ket. His "fur" is painted tiger skin and his mask a grimacing replica of the large striped cat. His movements also differ; his gait is more of a slinky sashay than a waddle. But he is no less holy for his stripes. The umbrella is held over him to denote this very sacredness.

Opposite: Barong dance at Batubulan. In this spectacular dance, performed daily for tourists, Rangda the witch emerges from behind the curtain on stilts, denoting her status. She is flanked by her flamboyant demon helpers.

Protectors of the Village

The Barong is one of the best-loved creatures by Balinese and visitors alike. With big eyes, clacking jaws and layers of "fur," he never fails to amuse. Yet, to the Balinese, the Barong is not just entertainment, he is one of the most sacred masks and dances. The Barong is the protector of the village. Not only does he stave off dark magical forces, he also restores balance in individuals and communities. Every 210 days, during Galungan festivities, many Barong roam the streets and dance in front of homes (*ngelawang*), bringing blessings and curing sickness. When a Barong dances, or even when brought out of the temple, villagers kneel down in reverence as he is considered a deity. This is not simply a playful creature.

His counterpart, Rangda, is the witch-widow and Queen of Black Magic. Her appearance is more frightening than the Barong, She has a long tongue dripping fire, flames shooting out of her head, long pendulous breasts and hair down to her knees. She carries a white cloth with sacred drawings on it that some Balinese say can cause illness by its very touch. Rangda is also revered, not out of fear, but respect. While she rules over the Pura Dalem (Temple of the Dead) in every village as the goddess Durga, she also brings balance to the world by transforming chaotic and demonic forces into benevolent entities.

History of the Barong

The origins of the Barong are vague. According to one account, around the thirteenth century a Chinese lion dance was seen on the southern shores of Bali, perhaps because a Chinese schooner had hit the reefs there. The villagers created their own version of the lion creature, which they named Barong Ket. For the Chinese, their Barong Sai serves the same function.

Mythological Origins

The mythological origin of the Barong is found in the *Lontar Barong Swari*. The god Siwa is ill and asks his wife Uma to descend to earth to find milk from a special cow. After weeks of searching, she finally finds the cow. The cowherd is willing to give her the milk in exchange for sexual favors. He is, in fact, Siwa in disguise, testing Uma's loyalty. Distraught, Uma finally relents, desperate for the medicine. Upon her return to heaven, she is cursed by Siwa and banished to earth where she becomes Durga, Queen of Black Magic. In meditation, she garners her powers, and faces the four directions to create plague and pestilence. This pleases the *bhuta kala* (spirits of chaos). The three supreme gods of heaven feel compassion for all the human suffering and come down to earth to cleanse it. Brahma descends as Topeng Bang (a red mask or Jauk, symbolizing a demon), Wisnu as Telek (a white mask symbolizing the gods), and Iswara as Barong. They cleanse the world by going from door to door and performing to disperse disease and pestilence.

Some say the etymology of the word Barong is from the Sanskrit *bharwang*, which means "two spaces" and could refer to the two places for the dancers in the Barong costume. Linguistics aside, the Barong closely resembles the Kala Bhoma head which adorns many temple and palace gates. This is Barong as Banaspati Raja (king of the forest), and indeed the carvings have foliage at the sides of the face.

Costumes

The Barong costume is quite impressive. Weighing about 40 kilos (90 pounds), it consists of a bamboo and wooden frame draped with *praksok*, the leaf fiber of a tree belonging to the pandanus family. Some Barong have crow or peacock feathers instead of fiber and are quite beautiful to watch. On top of the "fur" are a number of tooled leather pieces with shiny mirrors which catch the light. Two men dance, carrying the Barong. The man at the back can only see his partner's front legs, so he relies on musical and kinesthetic cues (from the front legs) to figure out what to do. The dancer in front manipulates the mask that is held in both hands by two wooden extensions protruding from the back of the jaw. It requires incredible physical stamina to dance the Barong.

For Rangda, the role itself, more than the costume, is what is weighty. The mask and headdress weigh close to 10–12 kilos (25–30 pounds), but the magical burden upon the dancer is of utmost importance. With long pendulous breasts, tresses of goat hair, fur pants and gloves and elongated fingernails, she is a formidable character. Her long tongue symbolizes an insatiable hunger. She is always after a victim to kill and use for her magical gain. Flames sprout from her tongue, symbolizing a merciless fire. Her bulging eyes show anger and fierce spiritedness. She is always putting herself forward and does not believe that anyone else has as much power as she does. Her fangs show an animal character, wild and fierce. On top of her hair are flames (*swidwara*) to reflect her magical and spiritual powers. To play the roles of Barong and Rangda, a dancer must undergo the cleansing *mewinten* ceremony. The dancer who plays Rangda, must be able to withstand attacks from

people in the audience who may want to "test" the power of the dancer by casting magical spells on him.

Rangda not only symbolizes the Queen of Black Magic or a witch but any powerful entity within a play, such as Siwa in both Legong Semaradhana (see p. 79) and the "Frog Dance" (p. 99).

When sacred masks are being carved, they are placed between the mask-maker's feet, considered spiritually unclean. Thus, before a Barong or Rangda dances for the first time, a special *melaspas* ceremony must take place to purify and sanctify the masks and costumes. Until this is done, the masks are considered "empty," nothing more than decoration. The next ritual is called *pasupati*, in which the masks are "married" to the rest of the costume so that they function as a personification of magical power. The third step is *ngerehin*, in which a number of villagers stay with the masks overnight in the graveyard, praying and presenting fruit and flowers. A priest speaks special incantations over the masks to empower them as protectors of the village. After this ceremony, they are enshrined in one of the village temples, usually the Pura Dalem situated near the cemetery.

The magical power of the Barong is in its face or mask, especially the beard, which is usually made from human hair. If calamity hits the village, the beard of the Barong is dipped in water, rendering the liquid holy and powerful for use in healing. Certain Barong and Rangda masks are more *sakti* (magically powerful) than others and often induce trance states in those who wear or come in contact with them. These masks are frequently "re-energized" with holy water, prayers and offerings.

Magical Significance

In Bali, Barong and Rangda are treated as deities. Their names show this: Dewa Ayu (Lovely Deity), Ratu Gede (Great or Esteemed One), Ratu Ayu (Great Beauty). When brought out of their resting place in the temple, the masks must always be carried on someone's head; they can never touch the ground (the Barong's beard sometimes touches the ground during his dance). When not in use, they are covered with a white cloth drawn with *rarajaban* (sacred symbols) to ensure the sanctity of the mask. Nearly every village owns at least one mask with full costumes.

The Barong is also an intimate part of every

Balinese in the form of the Four Siblings (*kanda pat*), which at birth are manifested as the placenta, amniotic fluid, blood and vernex on the baby. These Four Siblings protect the person throughout her or his lifetime, changing names. One of the *kanda empat*, the placenta, is the Barong himself, called Banaspati Raja (King of the Forest). If one's *kanda pat* are not intact or in balance, sickness results.

Rangda and Barong in Performance

The main role of Rangda and Barong in a performance-ritual is to re-establish balance. Rangda epitomizes black magic and destruction, Barong white magic and protection. They confront one another and fight but neither wins. Rather, a balance is struck for the moment. The Balinese acknowledge that negativity exists in each of us and is manifested as *bhuta kala*. Rangda rules over these spirits as well as human

The Barong Ket with one of his followers. As the protector of the village, the Barong must ensure that his charges do not get out of control. When they take the *keris* and stab themselves, the Barong comes round to help bring them out of trance.

Right: Trancers with Rangda. Here, the Barong followers are mesmerized by Rangda's power and are readying themselves to rush and stab her.

beings who can transform themselves into *leyak* (witches). The Barong, on the other hand, has human followers who often go into trance and try to protect him by rushing at Rangda with their *keris*. Her magical power is so strong that they turn their daggers against themselves (*ngurek*, *ngonying*) as an act of spiritual devotion (*ngayah*). Trancers feel an intense itching, usually around the heart/chest area, that has to be stabbed to be relieved. Even when they fall on their *keris* or stab themselves in the jugular, there usually is no injury or blood spilled. The power of the Barong protects them, they claim. In trance, they are impervious to injury or pain. The person is sprinkled with holy water to be brought out of trance. It is rare to see women go into a *keris*-bearing trance, except at the Pengerebongan ritual in Kesiman (see pp. 74–5) and at the Calonarang in Bitra during temple festivals.

Calonarang, a Tale of Magic

Many stories involve Rangda and Barong. The most common is *Calonarang*. Based on historical fact, this eleventh-century tale tells of Erlangga, son of the Balinese King Udayana and his Javanese wife, Queen Mahendratta. Angry with her husband for breaking his promise to her by taking a second wife, she kills him with black magic. Erlangga's father exiles the widow-witch (Rangda) to the forest with her infant daughter, Ratna Manggali. When the daughter grows up into a beautiful young woman, no one will marry her for fear of her mother. So Rangda devastates the land with famine, destruction and death.

Overwhelmed, Erlangga calls upon his spiritual advisor, Mpu Bharadah, for advice. One of Mpu Bharadah's pupils, Bahula, is advised to marry Ratna Manggali to discover the secret of her mother's black magic. He finds that Mahendratta has a book of sacred verses and recites the incantations backwards to wield her evil power. Having discerned her secrets, Mpu Bharadah challenges Rangda and destroys her. He then brings her back to life with the stipulation that she cease practicing black magic, a promise she cannot honor, for evil can never be eliminated.

The Performance

In this dance-drama, the Barong performs a 20–30 minute prelude to the story. Matah Gede ("Big Unripe One") is another name for Rangda, in her human form, referring to the incompleteness of her magical transformation into a witch. The first scene shows her in her human form, instructing her *sisya* (students) in the black arts. Ratna Manggali and her Condong (maidservant) appear and the story unfolds. Ratna Manggali unburdens her heart to her maid, lamenting that no one will marry her.

They exit and two servants of the king appear. They discuss the epidemics plaguing the country and reveal that the king will send his minister to kill the witch. Taskara Meguna comes onstage to carry out the order. All exit, and the *sisya* come on again, but this time they have transformed into witches, brandishing magical white cloths, their hair loose and disheveled. Calonarang appears, commanding them to go and kill the villagers. They exit.

The scene changes to the graveyard where the villagers are burying dead babies (dolls). When a baby

Matah Gede ("Big Unripe One") in her human form before she becomes a full-grown witch. This role is always performed by a man wearing elaborate make-up.

73

The monkey is the playmate of the Barong, offering him food, distracting him so that the monkey can finish the banana off by himself. He delights the crowds.

Telek performance. Around Galungan in Jimbaran, the *mepajar* ritual is staged. Part of it has the Telek dancers preparing for battle with the Jauk, or demons.

dies, the family must wait in the cemetery to ensure that witches do not steal the the corpse to use in order to incur more black magical power. In the play, this is a scene of comic relief. A papaya tree is planted in one corner of the stage space to represent the *kepuh* tree commonly found in cemeteries. Male clowns, portraying the villagers, lie down on a mat. Celuluk, one of Rangda's witches, known to be a nymphomaniac, creeps up when the men fall asleep. She approaches and fondles them. Thinking that they are dreaming of their wives, the men caress her back. One wakes, sees Celeluk and a hysterical chase takes place.

In some villages, a false corpse (*bangke-bangkean*) is brought in at this point. This is a very magically powerful man wrapped in a death shroud and carried on a platform into the performance area by a group of villagers. The bier, carried in a wild procession, is accompanied by a Gamelan Angklung or Balaganjur (the traditional music used in a cremation procession). A ritual is performed and the false body is taken to the village graveyard nearby. Here the man who acted as the corpse stays until dawn (usually only a few hours away), all the while being tested for his ability to ward off the presence of black magic.

Taskara Meguna now appears to challenge Rangda, who is in a makeshift elevated room at the side of the stage. He rushes up the bamboo ramp, dagger drawn, and forces Rangda out. The Rangda actor often goes into trance and runs into the graveyard, not far off. Villagers overcome by the power of the mask also fall into state. If there is no trance, then a dialog is held between Taskara Meguna and Rangda. Mpu Bharadah as the Barong enters and fights Rangda. The play ends with no victor. In true Balinese fashion, neither Rangda nor the Barong is pure evil nor pure good. One cannot exist without the other; they are two sides of an ancient coin.

Telek and Jauk

The Barong and Rangda are often associated with the masks called Telek or Sandaran and Jauk. Telek is a white mask with mother-of-pearl teeth in *alus* or sweet style. Jauk is a demon with bulbous eyes and buck teeth. His long, false fingernails are turtle shell sewn onto white gloves. The *alus* Jauk or Omang is white; the *keras* (strong) Jauk is red. Telek and Jauk dance in opposition to one another. Some say that Telek are gods and Jauk are demons, fighting over the elixir of life. Today, one can see these as separate dances (*tari lepas*) with four Telek dancing in unison or a solo Jauk dancer.

Sunda-Upasunda

This story tells of two brothers, Sunda and Upasunda, represented by Red and White Jauk masks, who both want to rule the three worlds. After receiving the power from God Brahma and a long self-sacrificing meditation, they decide to attack the heavens. To celebrate their victory, they call for a feast. While they are drunk, Brahma sends down a lovely *bidadari* (celestial maiden), Tilotama, to tempt the brothers. She succeeds and the two brothers fight one another to win Tilotama. Finally, they use their magic power to kill each other.

Pengerebongan

Every 210 days, a grand ritual takes place at the Pura Dalem Petilan temple in Kesiman, East Denpasar, where several different villages bring their Barong and Rangda masks to be blessed. All of the masks are "siblings" as they have been made from the wood of

the trees in this village's cemetery. Around 3 p.m., the temple complex is filled with worshippers and cockfighters. Cockfights take place in the big *wantilan* hall. The festive atmosphere has an undercurrent of tension. After all the masks have arrived, the people pray and within minutes a number of them fall into trance. The men must be restrained by at least two friends whereas the women are more subdued.

All the villagers and the Rangda and Barong masks circumambulate the *wantilan* three time, those in trance all the while grabbing *keris* and stabbing themselves. Many of the people wearing the Rangda and Barong masks are in a deep trance.

Later, a dance is done by older women of the congregation and some priests. Descending the steep inner steps, they sweep their arms to the side and up again, their feet criss-crossing as they progress forward. Dressed in an older style of clothing, they weep in front of a council of elders. Everyone is then brought out of trance, and the Rangda and Barong masks are taken back to their respective villages.

The Batubulan Barong Dance

Most visitors see the commercial version of Barong and Rangda in Batubulan village, done daily at 9.30 in the morning. There are wonderful depictions of witches in animal-like guises and a bit of off-color humor. If time is limited, this is a good venue to see Balinese theater. But for a real treat, try to see the Barong and Rangda in a ritual performance at a temple festival.

Different Types of Barong

Usually the Barong Ket comes to mind when people mention the Barong, yet there are many other types. The Barong Macan is a tiger, whose body is made out of striped cloth; the *naga* is a serpent; the *asu* or dog is found in the area of Baturiti; the *bangkal* is a boar; the *bangkung* a sow; the *gajah* an elephant; the *singa* a lion; the *lembu* a cow, and the *dawang-dawang* or *blas-blasan* are Wayang Wong masks.

The oldest is Barong Berutuk found only in Trunyan (Kintamani). However, Tirta Sari's show on Friday nights in Peliatan features a Berutuk facsimile. The Berutuk ritual is a rite of passage for the young men of Trunyan and a re-enactment of the founding of this village by the ancestors Druwene or I Dewa

Pancering Jagat (Lord Root of the Universe) and Druwene Luh or I Dewa Ayu Pingit (Forbidden Goddess). The masks are crudely carved from wood or a coconut. The costumes comprise hundreds of strips of dried banana leaves tied around the waist and neck.

Barong Landung

Another type of Barong is Barong Landung. Larger than life, these 3-meter-high puppets are each danced by one man. The performer's mouth and eyes are at the bellybutton of the puppet. These are common in Gianyar and Badung regencies. At the full moon in October, they parade down Hayam Wuruk Street in Denpasar.

One of the origin stories of the Barong Landung dates to the twelfth century. King Jayapangus of Kintamani married a Chinese princess and the two main puppets are thought to be these characters. The two most important puppets are Jero Gede, a black-faced unkempt male, and his wife Jero Luh, white-faced with Chinese features. In some villages, the family is completed with three smaller puppets, their children. When the puppets are "danced," they sway from side to side. A small drama is enacted wherein the two puppets tease one another. They speak in prose and poetic forms which are a combination of *macapat* (four-syllable rhyme) and folk songs. The stories used are from the *Babad* (Balinese Chronicles) and popular folk tales. This type of Barong is also considered sacred and exorcistic in nature.

The costume of the Barong Landung is a bamboo or rattan frame covered with burlap and clothed. Jero Gede wears a black shirt and a black and white checked *kain poleng* (skirt) while Jero Luh wears a white *kebaya* (blouse) with a colorful *kain* and sash.

In Banjar Gunung, West Denpasar, the Barong Landung are danced every 35 days outside the temple, and every Galungan (which occurs every 210 days) they are taken around the village. The musical accompaniment is similar to the gamelan used in Arja performances. Regular ritual performances (usually every 15 days on *kajeng kliwon*) are done in Banjar Intaran in Sanur; Banjar Sima, Sumerta Kaja in East Denpasar; Pekambingan in West Denpasar and in Banjar Taensiat and Banjar Krandan, Dauh Puri, Denpasar. In Dauh Puri, unlike in other places, women dance the role of Jero Luh.

Barong Landung Jero Gede and Jero Luh being blessed at a temple ceremony.

Barong Berutuk, one of the oldest Barong forms in Bali. The costume is made of dried banana leaves tied around the neck and waist.

Legong, Dance of Exquisite Beauty

The quintessence of femininity, Legong is one of Bali's most exquisite dance forms. The name derives from *leg* meaning "elegant movement" and *gong* for the music. Almost 200 years old, this dance was intended for performance by prepubescent girls who symbolized divine celestial angels. Tightly bound in gold-leafed costumes, the girls perform in unison, the flower trees of their headdresses quivering with every movement and shake of their shoulders.

The sacred Legong Ratu Dedari performed at the Panca Wali Krama ritual held in Besakih temple in 1993.

The two Legong and Condong perform in front of a temple gate at Blangsinga.

History of Legong

Records indicate that Legong was already an established art form by 1811. In the *Babad Dalem Sukawati*, a genealogical chronicle of the court of Sukawati, it is written that Legong was created as the result of a vision that came to the eighteenth-century king, I Dewa Agung Made Karna, of dancing celestial maidens. Another version says that King Dalem Ketut brought nine masks of celestial maidens from Java centuries earlier. The dates are inconsistent but the story of the vision is part of the history. Not knowing what the nine masks were for, King Karna meditated for 42 days and nights in the Pura Payogan Agung in Ketewel village near Sukawati. In his vision, he saw celestial maidens performing a dance of exquisite beauty and refinement. When he woke, he called together the priest of the temple and the village headman and told them what he had seen. He then taught the villagers the divine music and the dance. This is said to be the beginning of the Legong dance.

Legong Ratu Dedari, Masked Legong

Legong Ratu Dedari, also called Topeng Legong or Sanghyang Legong (as the masks are named after the celestial maidens called Sanghyang Bidadari), is still performed today during the *odalan*, which falls on Pagerwesi in the Balinese calendar, at Pura Payogan Agung. It is an extremely sacred dance performed in the *jeroan* of the temple and cannot be photographed (the picture here was taken at Pura Besakih during the Panca Wali Krama ritual in 1993). The two girl dancers must be prepubescent and follow proscribed rules. Nine masks are kept in the temple, of which seven are danced. Each mask has a mouth piece that the dancer bites down on to keep it on her face. The masks are so holy that they cannot be touched, so the dancers adjust the masks with a small piece of cloth held in their right hands. The movements are the precursors to those of modern-day Legong.

Nandir, Legong Done by Boys

Sometime in the late nineteenth century, I Gusti Ngurah Jelantik (great uncle of A. A. Raka Saba, one of the great Legong teachers of the twentieth century) created a new dance similar to Legong Ratu Dedari called Nandir. The dancers were young boys, and masks were not used. When the King of Gianyar saw Nandir, he was so impressed that he commissioned a pair of artists from Sukawati to choreograph a similar dance for young girls of his court. This became the basis for Legong as we know it today. Unfortunately, Nandir no longer exists. One of the great Nandir dancers, I Wayan Rindi from Banjar Lebah in Denpasar, was also the first Condong (maidservant) dancer in 1928. This solo dance is attributed to Ida Bagus Boda of Kaliungu, Denpasar.

Legong Keraton

From the mid-1930s to the 1950s, new solo dances were created, all referred to as Legong for lack of specific terminology. Legong was renamed Legong Keraton (meaning "palace") to differentiate it from the others when it was taken to the *keraton* in Surakarta, Java, in the 1930s. Other dances became known as *tari lepas* ("free" dances or dances not attached to drama). One can still see a performance of the Legong dance today for tourists in which the actual Legong itself is not even done.

A new choreography of Legong using multiple dancers walks in procession for the anniversary of Denpasar city, 2004.

The Structure of Legong

Legong is essentially a pure dance in that the story is enacted through highly stylized movement. Structurally, Legong is composed of four or five parts: *papeson* (entrance), *pengawak* (main part), *pengecet* (elaboration of the *pengawak* in at least double the time), *pengipuk* (in some stories) and *pekaad* (ending).

In Legong Lasem, the first to appear in the introduction is the Condong or maidservant. A single girl dances abstractly, carving out the space in front of her with hand movements. She picks up two closed fans on the ground in front of her, and dances with them. The second section begins with two Legong dancing in unison facing the Condong. The fans are presented to the two Legong and the *bapang condong* begins—an energetic and strong piece with open fans. The Condong exits and the Legong story begins.

There are sixteen different pieces in the repertoire, although not all of them are remembered in their entirety. The *pengawak* is elegant and slower than the *papeson*, with the dancers moving through a symmetrically choreographed piece lasting for more than twenty minutes. In the *pengecet*, the tempo doubles. Facing each other, they dance in opposition. If a story is told, the dramatic action begins here. There may be a *pengipuk* or a "kissing" section for a love scene or there may be a fight (*pesiat*). Finally, in *pekaad* the dancers face first the audience, then downstage, and turn around slowly to take their leave.

Two Legong in *pengipuk* ("kissing"), a movement denoting seduction in the Legong Lasem.

Right: I Luh Nyoman Sulasih and Anak
Agung Isteri Sri Utari perform Legong
Untung Surapati. This Legong was choreographed by Guruh Soekarnoputra
for the Sekaa Gong Tirtasari Peliatan,
and performed at ARMA during the
1995 Walter Spies Festival.

A scene from Legong Jobog depicting
a misunderstanding between the twin
monkey brothers, Sugriwa and Subali,
over what happened after killing the
demon Mesa Sura at Kisena cave. The
branches in the dancers' hands symbolize the uprooted trees which the
brothers used as weapons.

Training

Traditionally, Legong was performed by prepubescent
girls whose supple bodies lent themselves gracefully
to the exquisite movements. Training began at a very
early age, and vigorous massage was a part of the
process. The dancers would look forward to a performance at the temple after the harvest and spend 6–7
months in hard rehearsal. Today's lifestyle is too
demanding to ask a young girl to practice 2–3 hours
a day. Until the late 1990s, it was difficult to find prepubescent girls studying Legong as they preferred
to study the easier and shorter *tari lepas*. With the
increased interest in classical dance today, however,
many of the *sanggar* (dance studios) are producing
top quality Legong performers.

The Power of the Headdress

The dancers are covered from head to foot in golden
silk-screened *kain* (skirt) and blouse, with many
leather ornaments covering the body that accentuate
their movements. The most distinguishing element is
the *gelungan* (headdress) made out of leather with
fresh frangipani flowers stuck into the body as well
as on "wire trees" (*bancangan*) that quiver when the
head moves. In some villages, these *gelungan* are considered sacred and are kept in a high and reverent
place in the shrines; some of them are even trance-
inducing. In the Pura Desa of Sumerta, Denpasar, for
example, there are four sets of specially blessed *gelungan*. During the *odalan* (on the tenth full moon, which
usually falls in April), more than a dozen young girls
come out to dance Legong. However, before comple-
tion many of the girls fall into a trance state. They
are constantly watched by the male constituents of the
temple, as the headdresses are not allowed to touch
the ground, as it would defile them. After the girls go
into trance, they are taken into the inner courtyard
where they are revived with holy water and offerings.

Legong Prabangsa

In Tista, Kerambitan, a different kind of trance occurs. Legong Prabangsa begins with the dance of the
Condong. Then the two Legong enter and dance the
roles of Prince Prabangsa and a messenger from an
enemy court. When the messenger goes offstage, he is
replaced by a male dancer wearing the costume and
mask of the witch Rangda, who is Prabangsa's enemy.

The Legong dancer remaining onstage pulls out a
keris, goes into trance and starts to stab the witch.
This angers the onlookers so much that many of them
fall into convulsive trance and try to kill the witch
with their daggers. In the end, no one wins.

Repertoire

Legong that are still commonly performed include:

Bapang. This is the name of a *gending* or song. It
is a very strong dance that is often used as a warm-up
for the Legong. The dancers must be able to perform
both strong and refined movements.

Candra Kanta. This story of the moon and sun is
part of the repertoire in the village of Saba, Gianyar.

Guak Macok. According to the late Nyoman
Rembang, this story is about a kind of red-eyed bird
who never lays her eggs in her own nest. One day, as
she is roosting on her egg in a crow's nest, the mother
crow arrives with food for her young and sees this
stranger in her home. A fight ensues. The dancers
use their arms like wings, looking for the eggs.

Jobog. The monkey brothers Subali and Sugriwa
are fighting over the celestial maiden Dewi Tara.
Remembering their skirmish when they were young
and in the lake, their anger explodes. They uproot
trees and hit each other with them.

Kuntir. This means "small" and is about the brothers Arya Bang (Sugriwa) and Arya Kuning (Subali)
when they were young. Their mother owned a *cupu
manik* (magic jewel box). She gave it to Subali but
his brother tried to take it from him. While they were
fighting over it, it fell and turned into a lake.

Kuntul. Two rice paddy birds play in the fields
while looking for food.

Kupu-kupu Tarung or **Tarum**. This shows two
butterflies playfully fluttering around.

Lasem. Princess Langkesari is lost in the woods of
King Lasem. He kidnaps her and tries to seduce her,
to no avail. Her family wages war on him via a bird
of ill omen. This piece is the one most often performed today.

Legod Bawa (also called **Linggodbhawa**). The gods
Wisnu and Brahma vie for power with the god Siwa.
Brahma says he is the most powerful and dons a
Garuda bird mask, while Wisnu claims he is the
strongest and transforms himself into a boar. Siwa
turns into a linga (phallic symbol) with no ends.

Wisnu burrows down to find the root while Brahma flies up to find the tip, but they are defeated by Siwa's greater power.

Pelayon. Most dancers say that this Legong has no story, but according to Ni Ketut Reneng, one of the greatest Legong of all time, who passed away in 1993, this is the story of Langkesari when she was young.

Prabangsa. The minister Prabangsa goes to kill the witch Rangda. The two *legong* re-enact a scene of a king and his adversarial minister. The king exits and a male dancer in a Rangda costume then comes onstage. The Prabangsa figure tries to kill Rangda with her *keris*, but is unsuccessful. The Legong dancer and many of the villagers then go into a violent trance. This is done in the village of Tista, Kerambitan.

Semaradhana. This is the story of Semara and Ratih, the god and goddess of sexual love. The heavens are being disturbed by the demon giant Wiraludraka, who can only be defeated by a half-man half-animal creature. The only deity capable of creating such a creature is Bhatara Siwa, who is in deep meditation and has to be wakened by Semara. Ratih weeps as she fears that Semara may be killed by Siwa. Semara cheers her up and they make love before he leaves. When Siwa wakes and opens his eyes, he sees Semara and burns him with his Third Eye. Ratih begs for forgiveness but Siwa reduces her to ashes as well. In the dance, one Legong becomes a wise man who tells Semara that he must shake Siwa out of his meditation. The two Legong become Semara and Ratih. Semara wakes Siwa, who turns into Rangda the witch in his anger.

Sudarsana. Created by I Gusti Agung Raka in the 1970s, it a story of black magic inspired by the *Calonarang* legend.

In Legong Lasem, King Lasem (above) attempts to seduce Princess Langkesari but she rejects him (below), using her fan as a shield. This is one of the most popular scenes from this well-known story of Javanese royalty.

Baris, Dance of the Warrior

With his mountain crown of shells, *keris* (dagger) and strips of golden cloth enveloping his small body, the solo Baris dancer cuts a fine figure. Ever on the look-out for imaginary enemies, his eyes dart up and down, left and right. This form shows in both abstract and realistic movements the bravery of the young warrior. In the ritual Baris Gede, actual spears, bows and arrows and other weapons are used in a group mock battle.

Warrior Dance

Baris encompasses both ritual and non-ritual dance forms. Ritual Baris includes mimed warfare performed by groups of male dancers bearing different weapons. Non-ritual Baris is a solo. Baris dance integrates dynamic and forceful movements, some rather stylistic and abstract, others derived from the martial arts. It probably originated as a symbol of the soldiers protecting the king in his palace. The historical Javanese poem "Kidung Sunda" (1550) tells of seven types of ritual Baris performed at cremation ceremonies in East Java. There are no less than thirty different kinds of ritual Baris in Bali today.

The word *baris* comes from *bebarisan* meaning "line." In ritual Baris there are many lines of dancers. The non-ritual form of Baris Melampahan is a dramatic form in which a number of men perform the Baris solo in succession as a prelude to episodes from the *Ramayana* or *Mahabharata*. All of the characters are infused with the heroic fervor characteristic of the Baris. This is not commonly seen today.

At the turn of the twentieth century, a new form called Baris Tunggal was created. This solo warrior dance is full of swirls of color and electrifying movements. Traditionally, this is the first dance learned by young boys, as the movements and strength they gain carries over to all the other forms.

Movements in Baris Tunggal

Baris Tunggal is usually featured as an introductory dance for a secular performance or sometimes in a dance-drama as a lead figure. Almost always performed by a young boy, occasionally a young girl, he becomes a warrior. He stakes out his territory, checking for enemies in all directions and showing off his prowess. The choreography is an A-B-A form; it begins with a *gilak* (a four-beat musical phrase) followed by a *bapang* (an eight-beat musical phrase) and concludes with another *gilak*. The dance is strenuous as it requires the dancer to hold his shoulders close to his ears and keep his arms in an upright, bent position for the duration of the piece, about fifteen minutes.

The dancer improvises by arranging a set of movements to his liking. It is very important for the drummer and the main *ugal* (metallophone) player to pay close attention to the dancer's signals for changes in movements. *Seledet* or darting eye movements to the side and back to center are used extensively in Baris and are linked to the musical phrases. A brilliant Baris Tunggal dancer must know the music very well.

Unlike Baris Gede which allows for variants in the costuming, Baris Tunggal only uses multiple layers of

Baris performed by Dayu Basmiari from Geria Tubuh, Abang, Karangasem. Baris is usually performed by young males, but here a young girl is able to capture the movements with ease.

colorful cloth strips (*awiran*) that hang from the torso and seem to envelop the dancer as he twirls around on one foot. Baris is identified by its unique pyramid-shaped headdress with small pieces of *cukli* (mother-of-pearl) shells. The headdress indicates dignity, heroism and purity due to its white color.

Ritual Baris

Baris Upacara (ritual) or Baris Gede (large) is performed by a large group of men. The movements are relatively simple, even crude in nature, with the dancers intermittently uttering short bursts of unintelligible sounds. Most forms are learned by direct participation as opposed to long rehearsal. The ritual Baris can be seen in certain villages such as Kintamani and Sukawana (Bangli), Sebatu and Tampaksiring (Gianyar), Sanur and Tanggun Titi (Denpasar), Tejakula (Buleleng) and several places in Tabanan, including Wongaya Gede. This type of Baris can only be performed for temple ceremonies, cremations or full moon rituals.

The function of Baris Gede dances is to enrich and complete a ceremony. The most important variants are Baris Tumbak, enacting a battle with long lances; Baris Dadap, performed with shields; Baris Presi, with dancers carrying a shield and dagger. This Baris is found in Bangli and Buleleng. In Baris Pendet, usually performed late at night in the inner temple courtyard, the dancers carry offerings. In Bangli and Buleleng, the Baris Panah is performed with bows and arrows. In Baris Bajra, the dancers carry tridents; in Baris Tamiyang, found in Bangli and Buleleng, the dancers hold shields; and in Baris Bedil, they carry rifles. In Baris Kupu-kupu, found in Renon and Banjar Lebah (Denpasar), dancers wear butterfly wings. The Baris Goak is a battle between soldiers and crows, found in Pulasari and Selulung (Kintamani). Baris Jangkang uses long lances, and in Baris Cina, done only in Renon, the dancers carry swords and move in martial arts formations.

One of the more interesting forms is Baris Ketekok Jago, performed at the cemetery during a cremation ceremony. Two lines of dancers, wearing distinctive black and white checked cloths draped over their shoulders like wings, dance first in a militaristic fashion while carrying lances. Then the dancer at the head of the line goes to each kneeling dancer in turn and

Baris dancer Anak Agung Gede Anom Putra from Ubud twirls, sending the layers (*awiran*) of his costume into a spin to indicate the end of a part of the dance or the entire dance. Manipulation of the costume is an integral part of Balinese dance.

I Gede Radiana Putra performs Baris. It is imperative for the dancer to control his emotions through his eyes. Widening the eyes (*nelik*) and shaking the shell-covered headdress is a typical movement in this dance form.

Holding the *awiran*, Anak Agung Gede Anom Putra of Ubud elongates the movement of his arm.

Above right: Baris Bedil at Bangli. A variety of weapons are used in the ceremonial Baris dances. Here, wooden rifles are brandished.

Below: Baris Gede at Batur. When Mount Batur, visible in the background, erupted in 1994, the local dancers performed Baris Gede to appease the gods.

Opposite right: Baris Poleng at Tabanan. The checkered material in the dancers' costumes gives the dance its name (*poleng*). This dance is only done at cremations.

Opposite below: Baris Tameng at Tejakula Buleleng. Wearing the *sesaputan* style of costume (as in Gambuh dance-drama), instead of the strips of *awiran* usual to Baris, each dancer carries a shield (*tameng*) and *keris*.

"kisses" him while spreading his "wings." It is one of the most poignant movements in Balinese dance, as if he is kissing farewell to the soul of the deceased. This movement actually describes a crow stealing eggs from a swan's nest, resulting in a battle.

Trance and Baris Gede in Sanur

In Sanur, Baris Gede involves trance. During the *odalan* (temple festival) of Pura Dalem Kedewatan in Sanur, a large procession departs from the temple mid-afternoon and goes to the sea in front of the Grand Bali Beach Hotel where the Baris dancers and the sacred Barong and Rangda masks are blessed. On the way back to the temple, a number of the worshippers (including women) and the dancers fall into a trance. Back at the temple, the 12–16 Baris dancers perform a mock combat until many succumb to trance and are taken into the inner courtyard.

Musical Accompaniment

Most solo dynamic Baris is accompanied by Gong Kebyar but the ceremonial Baris, which is more dignified in nature, is accompanied by Gamelan Gong Gede. A few variants of Baris Gede also use Gamelan Angklung and Gaguntangan as the accompaniment. Baris Cina uses Gamelan Gong Bheri (see p. 29). Regardless of its medium, the music for Baris is characterized by a relatively short melodic line called *ostinato*, usually in four- or eight-beat cycles and accentuated by drums and gongs.

Arja, Sung Dance-Drama

Romantic comedy at its best, Arja provides hours of entertainment. Dating back to the early nineteenth century, it uses stories from many eras. It is accompanied by a smaller and quieter gamelan, allowing the actor-singers to be heard above the tinkling of the music. Ribald humor within unconventional conventions, Arja invariably attracts a large crowd.

Mantri Manis, the refined prime minister in Arja, is often played by a woman, here Ni Wayan Murdi. Note her crown of frangipani flowers.

The four major clowns in an all-male Arja Muani, Denpasar, 2003. From left to right: Liku, Wijil, Desak, Rai and Punta.

Development of a New Form

Arja is a melodramatic operatic form integrating gamelan music, song, dance and storytelling; it features many comic and romantic scenes. Believed to have been created in 1825 for the cremation of I Dewa Agung Gede Kusamba in Klungkung, it has gone through periods of decline and revival since then.

At the beginning of the twentieth century, Arja emerged as a form of sung drama, incorporating material from popular culture. It was performed in the streets, not the courts. Known as Arja Doyong, it dramatized stories based on the *Malat* or *Panji* romances (eleventh-century stories of court life), as well as Balinese tales and Chinese and Arabic stories. Typical episodes revolve around a plot involving romantic intrigue, and often speak about karma (law of cause and effect). From the 1920s, female performers joined Arja for the first time in the Arja Rabi-Rabi.

At first, Arja was acted solely by males and fulfilled the need for lighter entertainment. During its second stage, it developed into a complex theatrical form combining music, dance and drama (Arja Gaguntangan) featuring both male and female performers. Artists adopted elements of the classical courtly art forms of Gambuh and Legong in order to enhance their plays. The tone range of Arja songs and dialog was enriched and greatly expanded by the inclusion of female performers. Both male and female social values and mannerisms were presented. The play appealed to both sexes, but predominantly to female audiences because of the romantic content of the stories.

Arja Gede

Arja established its present-day form during the 1940s with Arja Gede, when performers incorporated intricate vocal forms, stylized dance vocabularies, complex gamelan music and more ornamented and elaborate costumes. This was the first major Balinese theatrical form created outside the court and religious spheres. Since the 1940s, female actors have dominated the leading roles. Arja Gede established the norm of using stock characters, consisting of two or three maidservants, two sets of buffoons, two princesses, a queen, two princes and a minister. These characters can be divided into two groups: the protagonists, which include refined characters known as *manis* (sweet), and their opponents, featuring coarse and strong characters known as *buduh* (crazy). The scenes with *manis* characters are usually serious in nature, unlike those for the *buduh* characters, which are full of humor and slapstick.

The characters in Arja speak their lines by singing in a distinct way with stylistic recitation in Balinese. All *manis* characters sing their dialogue, which is translated into colloquial Balinese by their servants and attendants. In contrast, the *buduh* characters mostly speak their own lines so that translation is not necessary. Because of the dominance of singing, Arja is best accompanied by the sweet-sounding

Gamelan Gaguntangan with a large and small single-note bamboo zither (*guntang*). The leading melodic instruments are several *suling* (end-blown bamboo flutes), which elaborate the melodic lines of the singers. The ensemble also includes two small drums (*kendang*), a set of cymbals (*ceng-ceng*) and three gongs (*kajar*, *tawa-tawa* and *klenang*). In 1972, Arja performers at RRI (Radio Republik Indonesia) replaced the Gamelan Gaguntangan with Gamelan Gong Keybar, which had gained popularity because of the Gamelan Gong Kebyar competitions held in many places throughout the island (see pp. 24–5).

Primarily a sung drama, the skill of an Arja performer lies in being able to sing in the genre known as *tembang macapat* (a four-syllable line of poetry). There are normally seven types of songs used in Arja performances, each with its own meter, rhyming scheme and length. The dancer-actor must be able to improvise songs while simultaneously applying the specific guidelines for each type. For example, in *sinom* there are nine melodic lines, each with eight syllables except for the last line, which has twelve. Each line must end in a particular vowel sound; in this case, the sequence is a-i-a-i-i-u-a-i-a. Every character type has its own kind of songs. Since much of the dialog and singing is improvised, it takes great skill to perform correctly on stage. The singing itself resonates from the throat as opposed to the diaphragm and is very high-pitched.

All-Male Arja

In the 1970s, when the vernacular Drama Gong gained in popularity, Arja was almost abandoned because Drama Gong performance did not require the audience to know the songs to enjoy it. All characters in Drama Gong speak their lines. In the early 1990s, a new movement for Arja revitalization occurred in Denpasar, led by STSI alumni in the form of Arja Muani (all-male Arja, also known as Arja Cowok). This new Arja exploits the more humorous side of this form, making it immensely popular. The jokes are fast and furious. The body language, gestures and movements of the male actors, particularly those in cross-dressed roles, elicit great applause and laughter from the audience. These troupes are often booked out and perform all over the island. They are frequently seen on the local television stations.

Ni Nyoman Candri as the Condong in Arja. Candri is one of the more famous exponents of this dance.

Joged, Bali's Social Dance

She comes through the curtain smiling, her eyes bright. Scanning the audience, she spies her first dance partner for the night. Tapping him on the shoulder with her fan, he must oblige and dance with her. Bali's sole social dance, Joged Bumbung, is often performed at wedding celebrations as it brings lots of good cheer and laughter. The less frivolous Joged Pingitan involves only one dancer who performs all the roles in the black magic story of Calonarang.

Above and opposite: Ni Ketut Cenik in Joged Pingitan. This 83-year-old dancer can still mesmerize an audience. She dances all the roles of the Calonarang drama. Above, she plays with her fan in order to charm and invite the audience to dance with her. In the illustration opposite, she depicts Ni Rarung, one of Rangda the witch's devotees.

Joged or Joged Bumbung is the only form that might be called a social dance. A Joged troupe features 4–5 dancers, each of whom first does a short dance, twirling her fan and flicking her waist sash, her eyes searching the audience to find a good match. Her hips sway easily back and forth and her smile includes all her teeth, in contrast to the norm. (Balinese dancers in general do not show their teeth when smiling.) She can be sassy, sexy, languid or perky—a temptress or simply a really good dancer.

The Joged dancer will go into the audience and tap (*nyawat*) a man on the shoulder, who is then obliged to dance (*ngibing*) with her. Often he tries to run away as he does not want to embarrass himself in front of a crowd, but his buddies push him out onto the performing arena. He approaches the Joged, who wraps a *selendang* (sash) or *saput* (overskirt) around his waist. They then dance a duet. He tries to steal a kiss or two, sometimes a bit more in these daring times. A more intimate dance might ensue after the show. An excellent dancer shows off his abilities. A mediocre one just hams it up, trying to show his sexual prowess by being as macho as he can.

Balinese consider Joged a form of secular dance for weddings or the opening of a new enterprise. It always attracts a good crowd. Some Joged troupes are known for their pretty dancers while others for their vulgarity, quite popular among the young men.

Joged Bumbung at the Bali Arts Festival, Denpasar, 2003. Flirting with an audience member, this Joged dancer finds that the raunchier the moves, the more the audience appreciates it.

History

Joged dates back to the late nineteenth century in the village of Blahbatuh in Gianyar. At that time, the dancers were male and it was called Gandrung. In 1884, in the village of Sukawati, Joged Gandrangan, named after a dynamic musical piece with a "catchy" tune, was created with women dancers. Fifteen years later, Joged had spread to many other villages. It reached the peak of its popularity just after World War II, in Northwest Bali, where it was performed during the harvest and called Joged Bumbung after the bamboo tubes (*bumbung*) of the accompanying instruments (see p. 35). Today it can be seen everywhere, and is a popular dance in the tourist venues.

Leko, Joged's Cousin

Another form which combines movements from Legong and the *ngibing* from Joged is Leko, today performed only in Tunjuk (Tabanan), Sibang Gede (Badung) and Negara (Jembrana). The etymological origins of Leko are said to come from the name of a Chinese servant woman in Kintamani, Lae Khong. Reputed to be a fine dancer, she took movements from the Sanghyang Dedari and created a new dance.

Leko begins with two dancers performing one of the Legong stories. Their costumes are closer to the Legong style than Joged. Then they choose a partner from the audience to dance with. Leko is performed for harvest rituals, upon fulfilling a vow or for a temple ceremony. The gamelan consists of a number of *rindik* (bamboo tubes tied to a frame), drums and small gongs (see p. 35). However, in Tunjuk the gamelan is a five-tone *pelog* Semar Pagulingan.

Joged Tua, Dancing Happiness

In West Bali, a "new" type of Joged called Joged Tua ("senior") is performed by five dancers over sixty years old. This is a revival of on an old Joged group, first formed in 1958 in the village of Wongaya Gede, but disbanded in the early 1960s. Nang Yasman was the teacher for the group called Gamelan Grantang (bamboo tube xylophones struck by two mallets). Two drums, three flutes and a number of small gongs complete the ensemble. The dancers were all accomplished female teenage dancers.

In 2000, Nang Yasman, distraught because his wife had been ill for a long time, had a dream in which he was told that if he revived the old-style Joged, his wife would regain her health. So on 31 July 2000, the Sekeha Werdha Santa was brought back to life. Nang Yasman asked the former dancers to perform in order to ensure that the old style would be retained. According to Ni Wayan Kendri, one of the dancers, it was because none of the young women in the village wanted to learn it. She also said that the Joged was revived in order to bring harmony back into the world.

The first dancer to emerge from behind the curtains is considered to be *duwe* Pura Batukaru or to "belong to" the Batukaru temple and she is not allowed to dance with a partner. The next four dancers choose whoever they want to dance with and they often select women partners, something rarely seen, except in tourist venues. When these women perform, the years slip off and they dance with great joy.

Joged Pingitan, Solo Dance of Magic

Joged Pingitan tells the story of the great sorceress Calonarang. Some people say that this form dates to the turn of the twentieth century, when one of the Joged Gandrangan troupes went to perform in the village of Lebih, in Gianyar, a fishing village known for its black magic. While performing the Calonarang story, one of the dancers was struck by black magic and fell backwards in a faint. The musicians flew into a panic but the head of the troupe said, "Let's be calm. What if we take a flower from her headdress and throw it at the dancer? If she regains consciousness, we will honor the headdress and make it sacred. If she dies, we will throw the headdress into the ocean and disband the troupe." After the dancer was "hit" by the flower, a yellow butterfly fluttered around her head and she regained consciousness. This troupe gained great popularity and afterwards was known as Joged Pingitan.

In contrast to other forms, the Joged's partners are not allowed to dance vulgarly or to flirt with the dancer. The men instead must interact by means of formal dance movements. The word *pingit* means "forbidden" and refers to the fact that the Joged dancer cannot be flirted with. The headdress is covered entirely with white paper flowers and is considered sacred. Today, the greatest exponent of this form is Ni Ketut Cenik of Batuan, who is in her eighties, but still performs frequently.

Choral Forms: Janger, Cakepung and Genjek

Female and male choruses are used in temple rituals to call down the gods, but choral music as performance is a relatively new phenomenon. Janger is a way for teenagers to mix as they sing each other love songs. Cakepung and Genjek are performed by men sitting in half-circles, singing about their sorrows but with much gusto and laughter. The three forms share a common theme: the toil of everyday life in hardship and in love.

The crown of the female Janger dancer is like a fan and quivers when the dancer moves her head back and forth.

Janger dancers from Sanggar Warini at a royal wedding in Mengwi, 1999. The beginning of the Janger has the young girls and boys facing the audience. Songs of love and chastisement are the norm.

Janger, a Call and Response Dance

The word *janger*, meaning "being off-center," refers to the chaotic periods when this dance was at its peak. The dance dates to the late 1920s, but reached a peak in the 1940s and 1950s during the revolution against the Dutch, and before the attempted coup in 1965, as a tool for messages from various political parties.

Janger is more of a choral than a dance form. Ten to twelve pairs of young men and women face each other on the stage area, the men seated cross-legged, the women sitting on their heels. The women's songs originate from those used to bring Sanghyang dancers into trance, although the words have been greatly altered. The songs are often about love, although there also have been songs about patriotism, sports and about building peace in Indonesia during the turbulent post-Soeharto era. Often the young women tease the young men, asking them "where their handsome boys have been lately."

The men, called Kecak, chant nonsense words such as *kecak*, *byang* and *byuk* and tease the women.

The men's gestures are distinct to Janger: arms move rhythmically in front and fingers flutter; elbows rest on knees, heads on hands; fists smack palms; shoulders shrug. The women, by contrast, sway their bodies back and forth, twirl their fans and shift their heads from side to side while singing. Sometimes a play is inserted using stories such as *Arjuna Wiwaha*, *Gatutkaca Seraya*, *Sunda Upasunda* and *Legodbawa*.

Types of Janger

Janger in Kubu, Karangasem, began in 1920 from *matuakan* (palm wine drinking groups). The young people heard the joyful singing and made it into their own during harvest times. In the mid-1920s, I Made Keredek created and taught Janger in Kedaton, Badung, Peliatan and Singpadu. During this time, a *daag* (male dancer-singer) would lead the Kecak chorus. This is rarely seen today. In Sibang, Janger Gong is accompanied by a Gong Kebyar. In Metra, Bangli, a priest went into trance and was told to form a Janger troupe. Every fifteen days, on *kajeng kliwon*, this

youth group does a ritual called Janger Sanghyang Bobor. They go into trance and dance on coals formed of hot coconut shells.

The Janger gamelan, called Batel Jejangeran, consists of flutes, drums (*kendang*), cymbals (*ceng-ceng*), all of the small gongs (*tawa-tawa, klenang, kajar*) and a large circular frame drum (*rebana*). In some areas, metallophones (*gender*) are included.

Costumes

At first, Janger and Kecak dancers wore everyday clothing. Shorts, shirts with epaulettes, shoes and socks for the men could be seen in the 1930s in a similar form called Stamboel. The women would wear *kebaya* or long-sleeved blouses. Then both sexes began wearing temple clothes. The distinctive woman's headdress (*petitis*) is a modification of the wedding crown. Today, most Janger Kecak dancers wear a gilded cape (*saput*), headcloth (*destar*), large neckpiece (*badong*) and *kain* (long cloth) made out of traditional Balinese woven cloth. The Janger women wear gilded cloth from chest to ankles, beaded velvet neckpieces and leather armbands.

Cakepung, Mouth Music

The male Cakepung choral group is found only in Karangasem. It developed out of men in the neighborhood (*banjar*) socializing together in the village hall. A group of 10–20 men gather in a circle. A lead singer (*juru tembang*) begins to read from the palm leaf manuscript (*lontar*), reciting lines and songs from the *macapat* poetry tradition, while one of the others translates the words into more colloquial Balinese (a type of recitation called *cakepun*). One voice is the *pung* (timekeeping gong), thus the name *cakepung*.

A lead dancer improvises movements from Topeng, Gambuh or Kebyar in the center of the circle. One or two light musical instruments, such as a flute and bamboo zither, may be used to enrich the melodic line of the syncopated voices by the choir members, in both *pelog* and Sasak (Lombok) *slendro* scales. They sing nonsense sounds like *cak pung*. Performed in the cool of the evening, Cakepung is associated with harvest rites. As the night wears on, the singing gets rowdier as the men drink from a large container of *tuak* (palm wine)!

The story recited is *Tutur Monyet*, a version of

the *Panji* romance written in both Balinese and Sasak (Lombok) languages in the form of *macapat*. This vocal form has its roots in the seventeenth century in West Lombok. Some Cakepung performers in Budakeling village suggest that this became popular during the early decades of the twentieth century. The most active groups are in Budakeling, Sidemen, Padang Aji and Jasi.

Genjek, the Latest Vocal Craze

Another type of "mouth music" is Genjek, also found mainly in East Bali. Originally only a vocal form, today Genjek has added gamelan instruments, including a "gong" made out of two suspended bronze keys over a resonator, flutes, drums, and *tingklik* (bamboo xylophones). This newer form became popular in the 1990s, culminating in a Genjek festival at the Werdhi Budaya Art Centre in Denpasar in 1998. Numerous commercial recordings have also been made. Similar to Cakepung, Genjek tells no particular story. Home grown songs about how hard daily life is for the "little people" begin the performance. The men sit in a circle, passing around glasses of *tuak*, joking and clowning. Individuals stand in turn, singing the nonsense words *kesek, kesek, byos, byong, kapak de kapak* and moving their arms around each other in a web of friendship in this boisterous and joyful form.

In Peliatan, at the Mandala stage, one will find flashier costumes in their version of Janger.

The form of Genjek vocal music is incorporated into a new piece by the ARTI Foundation.

Kebyar Dances

Kebyar dances are distinctive in their abrupt transitional movements, quick shifts in tempo, high energy and the way the dancer interprets the music through facial expressions and body language. These forms first surfaced in the early twentieth century and have been developing ever since. The mood at that time was one of innovation, and choreographers used the opportunity to try new combinations and styles. Elements of both female and male forms were put together in one dance with the dancer expressing more than one style.

The distinctive positioning of the body (*agem*) in Oleg Tambulilingan has the female dancer leaning forward.

Opposite above: In Kebyar Trompong, the dancer, here Anak Agung Gede Oka Dalem from Peliatan, becomes a musician and intersperses playing the *reyong* with playing with his fan.

Opposite below: In Taruna Jaya, the solo dancer must be able to switch from being aloof to being flirtatious in just one gong cycle.

Below: Ida Bagus Oka Wirjana (73) from Blangsinga doing Kebyar Duduk. A student of the famous Mario, he developed his own style over 50 years ago.

Beginning of Kebyar Dances

The dynamism and range of emotional expression in Gong Kebyar also extends to dance. The first of these expressive dances, Kebyar Legong, was created in 1915 by I Wayan Praupan (also known as Pan Wandres) of Jagaraga. In this dance, two young men in *bebancihan* (cross-dressing costumes) performed in unison with a mixture of female and male movements taken from Jauk (the strong male masked dance), Leko or Gandrung (which is similar to the Joged social dance), Baris (the warrior dance) and Legong (the female court dance). Soon after its initial appearance, two young women began playing the roles. Most of the movements were executed in a sitting position, and thus the dance was also referred to as Kebyar Negak or the "sitting Kebyar dance."

The later Kebyar dances, Palawakia and Taruna Jaya, were strongly influnced by Kebyar Legong. The creator of these dances, I Gede Manik of Jagaraga, was one of the first dancers of Kebyar Legong which may explain why Palawakia and Taruna Jaya developed out of that dance.

From the 1950s, many other dances have been created in the Kebyar style (see pages 98–9), and the popularity of the genre shows no sign of abating.

Taruna Jaya, the Energy of Youth

I Gede Manik was a student of Pan Wandres and in 1952 he choreographed Taruna Jaya ("Victorious Youth") out of Kebyar Legong. At that time, it was danced by two women, but today it is usually done as a solo. This dance requires immense energy for the numerous changes in speed, dynamics and mood that the dancer must capture.

Taruna Jaya describes the many moods of a youth: coyness, bashfulness, irritability, sweetness, and, of course, energy. Strong eye movements are a prominent feature, and often include *nelik* (a wide-eyed stare). At one point, the dancer flings her extended *kain* to the side and sidles up to the drummer to flirt with him. He may either resist her advances or play along. The costume (usually dark purple) uses a headcloth with a unique shape, a long-sleeved tunic and a *kain* pleated on the left side with the end dangling. There are many moments when the dancer picks up the end of the cloth to emphasize a musical point or mood. She also uses a fan to its greatest advantage.

Sanggar Çudamani of Pengosekan has recently revitalized the version of Taruna Jaya composed by the late I Wayan Gandra of Peliatan. The dance can also be seen at venues performing dances for tourists.

Seated Kebyar Trompong and Kebyar Duduk

The famous dancer, the late I Ketut Maria, better known as Mario, went to Buleleng to hear the new Kebyar music sensation after seeing it performed in his home town of Tabanan in 1919. Invited to dance, he instead performed while seated at the *trompong*. He struck the knobbed gongs and played with his fan, and thus Kebyar Trompong was born.

In 1925, Kebyar Trompong developed into the magnificent Kebyar Duduk (seated dance), regarded as the quintessence of refined male dance. Dressed in an extended *kain* draped on the left side, which is often flung out, and wrapped from chest to hips in a gold-painted *sabuk* (long band), a slender young man flamboyantly twirls his fan. He emerges onto the stage, dances briefly then sits with one leg crossed over the other at the knee. He stays in this position for the rest of the dance.

The expression on the dancer's face is paramount: eyes dart back and forth, open wide and almost close completely while his head shifts effortlessly from side to side. A particularly difficult movement for the male dancer is when, with one foot tucked over the other in a kneeling position, he scoots around the stage. One of the greatest living exponents of this dance is Anak Agung Ida Bagus Oka Wirjana of Blangsinga (Gianyar) (p. 90, below).

Palawakia

This is another of Gede Manik's compositions which he created in the 1940s. A solo dancer sits behind the *trompong* and recites traditional poetry known as *kakawin* while simultaneously playing the instrument. Movements from the Topeng masked dance-drama are incorporated into the choreography, which consists of both standing and seated movements. This dance depicts a young man playing gamelan, but is usually performed by a young women. The poems she recites are taken from the *Mahabharata* and *Ramayana* epics.

Oleg Tambulilingan, Dance of the Bumblebees

The Bumblebee Dance was specially choreographed by Mario for two dancers from Peliatan for the village's dance company tour to Europe and the United States in 1952. I Gusti Rasmin Raka and I Wayan Sampih, then aged 13 and 22, were the first bumble-

bees. (Raka still dances today in special Seniman Tua (senior artists) nights.) It was the first time that women had raised their arms above their shoulders (when lifting the "wings"), showing their underarms, and thus it caused much controversy among the older Legong teachers in Peliatan at the time.

In the dance, a slender young woman comes onto the stage holding her "wings" (two long pieces of chiffon attached to her belt) in her hands, and mimes the opening of the dance curtain with fluttering fingers. Her *agem* (basic stance) differs from others in that her body protrudes more forward and her hands are held closer to the body. She frolics in the garden, flitting like a bee from flower to flower. A young male bumblebee appears, and they dance around one another, at last lightly embracing. The male dancer wears the same costume as a Kebyar Duduk dancer.

Kecak, Rhythmic Vocal Chanting

Circles of men, clad in black and white loincloths with a brilliant red hibiscus flower tucked behind their ears. Light from a tree of oil lamps illuminates their faces. A cacophony of sound, "*Cak, Cak, Cak*" in multiple rhythms, brings on the Kecak dance-drama. Born out of the male choruses accompanying the Sanghyang trance rituals, Kecak has become one of Bali's most well-known dances. In its new form, it is a secular dance performed exclusively for tourists.

I Made Sidia as the monkey king Subali, about to go into battle to challenge his brother Sugriwa.

Origins from Sanghyang

Cak or Kecak, one of Bali's most well-known performing art forms, integrates complex multilayers of rhythmic vocal chant, dance and drama. Known to the Western world as the "Monkey Dance," Kecak was developed in the 1930s by utilizing the vocal chant of Sanghyang, yet there is no trance in Kecak.

Kecak is often described as a form of *gamelan suara* (voice orchestra) and is named for the onomatopoeic sounds *cak* or *cek* chanted throughout the performance. This is enriched with melodic phrases and rhythmic patterns borrowed from gamelan. The sharp, short sound of *cak* makes it easier for chorus members to recreate the rhythmic effect of gamelan with interlocking voices.

The Rhythms

The polyrhythmic vocal chanting that makes up most of the performance is sung in interlocking parts. Most chorus members know at least four different rhythmic patterns: syncopated *cak telu* (three syllables), *cak lima* (five), *cak nem* (six) and the simple non-syncopated pattern *cak ocel* (three and seven syllables). There is also improvised *panyelah* (five syllables). Syncopated rhythms require three voices: *polos* (down beat), *sangsih* (upbeat) and *sanglot* (in between). The interlocking patterns of three and six strokes are chanted within one gong cycle and are marked in the melody by a gong-like sound, *sirrrrr*. The five-stroke and non-syncopated patterns are freer. All patterns are laid over the *kajar* and the melody. The *kajar* is the timekeeping gong, vocalized in Kecak with a *pung* sound. The melody is chanted as *yanger yangur yanger yanger yang sir*.

The Performance

Laid over the *cak* chorus is an excerpt from the *Ramayana*, usually "The Abduction of Sita" done in Sendratari style. The story is easy to follow (see pp. 40–1). The main attraction of Kecak is its multilayered rhythmic vocal chanting, the choreographic patterns the men make on the ground, and the atmosphere created. It is erroneously called "The Monkey Dance" because the chanters become Hanuman's

I Wayan Limbak, one of the original dancers of the Kecak, played the lead role in "The Death of Kumbakarna," a story used in early Kecak performances.

monkey army at one point during the show, but they also become trees, wind, fire, a magic serpent and many other non-simian images.

It is believed that Kecak is a relatively recent innovation of the Sanghyang tradition. I Made Sija, a master dancer and puppeteer of Bona, Gianyar, claims that Kecak was created before the Dutch occupation of Bali in the early 1900s. At that time, Bona and the surrounding villages were plagued by a serious epidemic which caused countless deaths. To ascertain the cause, a Sanghyang medium went into trance and revealed that the deities wished to have a form of music to dance to. The villagers spontaneously created vocal music by chanting the melody and rhythmic patterns imitating the *reyong* (set of kettle gongs) and *ceng-ceng* (cymbals). In the ritual, Cak helped induce an altered state of consciousness by repetition.

In this performance by the Kecak Puspita Jaya group from Blahkiuh, Hanuman gives Sita a ring from Rama to prove that he is an emissary from Rama.

Left: The Kecak circle. Rama and Laksmana are held captive by Meganada, son of Rawana. The *cak* dancers represent the magic weapon, portrayed as a *naga* serpent, which binds them in place.

Secular Kecak emerged in the 1930s, with two different accounts of its creation. In the 1920s, Bali resident Walter Spies was inspired by the emotional and dramatic intensity of the ritual Kecak chorus he saw in a performance of Sanghyang Dedari in Bedahulu (Gianyar). He suggested to the Balinese that they take the chorus of the Sanghyang and add scenes from the popular *Ramayana* epic; Spies later maintained that this newly created Kecak was a pure Balinese inspiration. The male chorus, wearing only loincloths, move their body in unison while sitting in concentric circles, chanting in rhythmic patterns. According to I Wayan Limbak, one of the original dancers, the story they performed in the beginning was "Karebut Kumbakarna" (The Death of Kumbakarna). He was chosen to play the lead role.

The second version claims that at about the same time, I Gusti Lanang Oka of Bona and I Nengah Murdaya created Kecak Ramayana by blending the vocal music (*kecak*) of the ritual Sanghyang with the *Ramayana* epic. Murdaya, who had just moved to Bona from Singaraja, used his knowledge of northern Balinese gamelan style to enhance the music of this newly created art form. The first performance enacted the story of Sita's abduction, still popular today.

Several other sources suggest that dramatic Kecak was created in Bedahulu and was later developed in Bona. Most dance experts in Bali, however, agree that Murdaya and Lanang refined the formal structure of Kecak. Kecak dancers from Bona later established Kecak troupes all over Bali.

Since the 1970s, a number of new versions of Kecak have emerged (see pp. 100–1). The latest innovation is Luh Luwih's all-female *cak* troupe, which performed at the 2004 Bali Arts Festival.

In the Kecak circle, the rhythmic chanting is elaborated by hand and arm movements. With over a hundred voices, a wonderful textured soundscape is created.

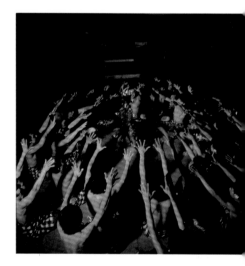

Dances of the 1940s to 1960s

The *bebancihan* style of cross-dressing reached its zenith in the 1940s and 1950s with the creation of a number of new dances, most about young men but performed by young women. These girls wear short, triangulated headgear with a piece of cloth more loosely draped around their hips than in the usual female styles. In the 1960s, dances depicting scenes from daily life, such as weaving and farmer dances, became the standard. In early 2004, a festival commemorated I Nyoman Kaler's creations in this style.

"Panji Semirang," a Kebyar dance performed by a Warini student in 1980. The typical *bebancihan* (cross-dressing) costume with an extended piece of material on the left side has not changed much since the 1940s.

The maestro of *bebancihan*, I Nyoman Kaler, is seen here teaching Ni Made Darmi in the 1940s.

Popularity of Cross-Dressing

The Kebyar style, which began in 1915, accelerated in its development in the 1930s. The intensity of the bold new sounds and the accompanying dances, filled with brisk and sharp movements, gained immediate favor with the Balinese. A new level of creativity was achieved during the 1940s and 1950s. *Tari lepas* (non-dramatic dances) in the Kebyar style appeared during this time and several are still popular today. Many are solo pieces that show off the virtuosity and musicality of the dancer. Others are duets or small group dances. *Bebancihan* dances with women in men's roles wearing refined male costumes became the vogue, bringing female dancers to the fore in an entirely new form.

I Nyoman Kaler's Creations

The late I Nyoman Kaler of Belaluan, Denpasar, was a prolific and innovative choreographer and composer, who created a number of works. "Margapati," a solo dance performed by a young woman, depicts the lion, king of the forest. The name comes from an opening movement in which the dancer squints her eyes and does an S-shaped movement with her neck and head to the right. This imitates the eye movements of a sleeping lion. Her costume consists of a *kain* (cloth) wrapped from her hips to just below the knees and pleated on the left to allow freedom to move her legs. The arms and shoulders are bare, and the hair upswept and tucked into a simple *gelungan* (headdress). In a distinctive movement, the dancer puts her hand on her breastbone with the elbow held out to the side, rolls her shoulder backwards, quickly followed by a *seledet* (darting eye movement to the side), like a lion eyeing his prey. This dance was choreographed in 1942.

"Demang Miring," also choreographed in 1942, refers to the Demang character in Gambuh. Two movements, called *tayog Demang* and *godeg miring,*

give the dance its name. These were combined with motifs from Legong Keraton. Parts of the music are similar to Kebyar Duduk. When the popular Ni Made Darmi married in 1957 and moved to Lombok, the dance declined in popularity.

"Panji Semirang," developed in 1943, has also been attributed to I Nyoman Kaler, although some say it was created by Wayan Lotring who composed the music. The story is of Candra Kirana, betrothed to Prince Panji in East Java. Separated from her beloved, she disguises herself as Panji and wanders the countryside in search of him. The costume is almost identical to "Margapati," but here the dancer uses a fan. The quick change from one *agem* (dance pose) to another is distinctive. There are usually one or more movements between each pose before the final *agem* is executed. Ni Luh Cawan, a famous Legong dancer in Badung, popularized this form.

"Cendrametu," also created in 1943, is a duet in which the dancers use fans to depict the full moon peeking out from the clouds. This dance is rarely seen today. Ni Luh Cawan and Ni Nyoman Sadri from Kelandis in Denpasar were the first dancers to perform this number.

"Wiranata" was created by I Nyoman Ridet in 1945. It depicts a strong and brave king character. A distinguishing feature is the *seledet*; the dancer must be able to move her eyes quickly and succinctly from side-to-side and to the upper corners in time to the music. Jero Made Puspa of Puri Satria in Denpasar, probably the best known dancer of this form, tells of submerging herself in the village river to practice the quick eye movements. Another distinctive movement is *tayog prabu* from the king in Gambuh.

"Bayan Nginte," created in 1950, is a solo dance which uses the flowing *selendang* (scarf) of Central Javanese dance to elongate the movements of the arms. I Ketut Merdana and I Nyoman Kaler had seen the elegant and stately classical Javanese court

dances in Central Java. Elements of Balinese and Javanese dance were fused into a new form. Part of the dance is done while seated on the ground.

Labor of Love

It was rumored that President Soekarno requested choreographers to create dances for and about the proletariat. The consciousness that arose from the influence of the Indonesian Communist Party (PKI) helped shape these dances. The choreographers were responding to the common people's wishes as opposed to those of the palace. Three dances created from 1958 to 1960 reflect this view.

"Nelayan" depicts fishermen casting out their nets, bringing in the fish and rowing their boats. I Ketut Merdana from Kedisan, Buleleng, choreographed this and composed the music in 1958. After a long hiatus, this dance is enjoying a revival among children's groups in Bali today.

"Tenun" portrays spinning thread, warping the loom and weaving. Performed by 3–5 women, most of the dance is executed in a kneeling position. The most distinctive part of the costume is the *lelunakan* (headcloth) worn by women in Badung. This dance was created by I Nyoman Ridet from Krobokan, Badung. I Wayan Likes, from the same village, composed the music in 1957. "Tani" reflects the work of a farmer. Mimetic movements show the furrowing of fields, planting of rice, shooing of birds and harvesting. The music and the dance were created by I Wayan Beratha of Abiankapas, Badung, in 1957.

In the early 1960s, a few more frivolous dances were created. One of these was "Tari Badminton" (badminton dance) by I Nyoman Kaler. It did not enjoy a long life at the court. One dance recently revived in Peliatan is Mario's "Sabungan Ayam" (cockfight dance) in which two men dressed as fighting cocks spar with one another.

Left: The "Candera Metu," an earlier form of Kebyar dance created by I Nyoman Kaler, is performed here by one of his prize students, Jero Made Puspawati (aged 73), at the Kaler Festival in Denpasar, 2004.

Center: Ni Made Darmi (aged 69) dances "Bayan Nginte," also choreographed by Kaler, in Denpasar, 2004. This dance fuses elements of central Javanese dance with Balinese Kebyar.

Right: Ida Ayu Wimba Ruspawati (left) and Ni Komang Puspadewi (right) performing "Kupu-kupu Taruna." This is a group dance depicting butterflies flitting around a beautiful, lush garden.

Sendratari and Drama Gong

I Wayan Retug and Pidada in a scene from Calonarang Bondres, influenced by Drama Gong.

The character of a Prime Minister in Sendratari, influenced by the classical dance-drama Gambuh. Here the prime minister's hands are in the position of listening to his king.

Sendratari was created in the early 1960s. A large troupe of dancers pantomime their roles while a *dalang* or storyteller recites the plot. This is a spectacular production with elaborate costumes and make-up, more popular with Balinese than with visitors as the entire play is in colloquial Balinese and the movements are more static. Drama Gong, so named as it is more of a stand-up, slapstick drama accompanied by a gamelan (gong), always draws a huge crowd. Like Sendratari, it is in colloquial Balinese.

Drama Gets a New Face

The most recent genres of drama have their origins in the establishment of the New Order government of former President Soeharto. There was a good deal of civic support for these forms at that time. Sendratari (an acronym for SENi DRAma TARI or the Art of Drama and Dance), is based on a similar form in Central Java. Sendratari uses no dialog between the actor-dancers on stage; rather, a *dalang* sits with the gamelan and recites or sings all their lines in both High and Common Balinese, readily understood by the public. The dancers combine pure movement and gesture to convey the story and portray their characters. When there is dialog among characters, the dancers utilize a lot of gestures and facial expressions underlined by the narration of the *dalang*. Some of the dramatic moods and actions are conveyed by a group of female singers (*gerong*).

Stories Used in Sendratari

The first Sendratari was choreographed and composed by I Wayan Beratha and produced by the Conservatory of Traditional Performing Arts (KOKAR, now known as SMKI or the High School of Arts) in 1960. This Sendratari Jayaprana re-enacted the tragic Balinese love story between Jayaprana and Layonsari. In 1965, Beratha created Sendratari Ramayana. Since then, this form has been warmly welcomed by the local populace. A number of Sendratari have followed, including the Balinese legends "Mayadenawa," "Sang Kaca," "Nara Kusuma" and "Gatotkaca Seraya" from the *Mahabharata*, and the Chinese love story "Sampik Ingtai."

Since 1979, the annual Bali Arts Festival has produced colossal Sendratari. The first was a collaboration of faculty, teachers and students of KOKAR and ASTI; subsequently, each school produced its own.

Costuming and staging run to the extravagant when this form is done on a large stage. In order to fill the enormous outdoor amphitheater at the Werdhi Budaya Art Centre in Denpasar, a Sendratari production requires more than a hundred dancers along with musicians playing multiple gamelan ensembles.

Influence of Sendratari

The popularity of Sendratari has significantly impacted other forms of performing arts. The emergence of the modern Drama Gong in the mid-1960s was greatly stimulated by Sendratari. The current Kecak Ramayana also was influenced by Sendratari Ramayana in dramatic scenes and costuming. Arja at some point featured characters from the Sendratari Ramayana in some of its performances.

It may be difficult for non-Balinese to understand the nuances of Sendratari due to the use of colloquial Balinese language. However, the style of this form can be seen at any Kecak and Ramayana Ballet shows done in commercial venues.

Drama Gong

In Drama Gong, every gesture and movement of the actors is tightly linked to the cues of the Gamelan Gong Kebyar. Although first created as melodrama, it has evolved into a comical soap opera accompanied by music. Since its inception in 1966, this form has enjoyed enormous success among the locals. Familiar Drama Gong stars now even sell goods in television and newspaper advertisements.

The name Drama Gong derives from its two most prevalent performance elements: drama (storytelling) and Gamelan Gong Kebyar. It draws performance elements and character roles from Arja, yet borrows many conventions from Western style modern drama as well, such as the use of a proscenium or thrust stage with static décor, painted scenery, modern lighting and realistic acting.

During the attempted coup and bloody aftermath of 1965, a number of great dancers were murdered. Thereafter, Anak Agung Gede Raka Payadnya, an actor-dancer from Abianbase, Gianyar, and a graduate of KOKAR/SMKI, felt it would be easier to find actors who were not classically trained dancers and singers. As popular theater, the stories speak to a wide audience rather than to an élite.

Drama Gong employs traditional gamelan music, the prominent use of vernacular Balinese language, and the presence of stock characters, usually stereotyped as either refined and sweet (*alus* or *manis*) and coarse or crazy (*keras* or *buduh*). The major roles are a king and his queen, two ministers (one wise, one greedy), a refined princess (Putri Manis) with her servant (Dayang), a refined prince (Putra Manis) with a pair of male servants (Punakawan or Panasar), a coarse prince (Putra Keras) with his two buffoons, and a crazy princess (Putri Buduh). There are also other roles, such as farmers.

The stories are derived from the *Panji* or *Malat* romances, well-known Balinese legends, as well as excerpts from the *Mahabharata* epic (see p. 41). The central theme is the struggle between good and evil, with good usually triumphing. More importantly, the plays, which are tragicomic in nature, contain moral teachings and other messages in addition to the romantic and endless comic scenes. In contrast to the older forms of Topeng and Arja, here the buffoons do not share the moral high ground of their masters; rather, they mock the airs of the royals.

Drama Gong troupes are hired for a variety of occasions: fundraisers during temple ceremonies, youth group activities and any number of other village events. The entire family comes out to see their favorite actors cavort on stage. There is also a weekly Drama Gong performance on the local TVRI station. For visitors, however, watching a Drama Gong is a test of stamina as there is little or no dance and the dialog is conducted exclusively in Balinese.

Putri Manis, a stock character in Drama Gong. The acting in Drama Gong is usually melodramatic and theatricalized.

The huge outdoor amphitheater, Ardha Chandra, at the Werdhi Budaya Art Centre in Denpasar is an ideal setting for spectacular dance-dramas.

Contemporary Dance and Drama Forms

To a Balinese, contemporary can mean anything dating back to the 1960s—something with a new twist choreographically, thematically or in costume. There are new performance pieces based on traditional movements, those combining elements of other cultures as well as real departures from the norm. These pieces are gaining more acceptance for they bring new aesthetic principles to the stage, such as minimalist costuming and musical accompaniment.

In "Cendrawasih," two birds of paradise frolic in a garden to express their love.

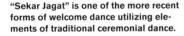

"Sekar Jagat" is one of the more recent forms of welcome dance utilizing elements of traditional ceremonial dance.

The Balinese both applaud and abhor change. Purists deplore any kind of tinkering with traditional movement or music. Contemporists embrace anything new, sometimes to the detriment of the form itself. Since the 1960s, a number of new dances have been created by local choreographers. Some are the result of innovation in existing traditional dance forms, others the result of combining elements of different cultures and the application of modern choreographic approaches to local art forms. Many new pieces are produced collaboratively among choreographers and composers in the Kebyar form of music and dance. Almost all of them are still bound to tradition in some way, either in their structure, form or concept.

Adapting Traditional Movements

This movement started with the creation of the secular "offering/welcome" dance of "Gabor," by I Gusti Gede Raka, a well-known Legong teacher from Saba (Gianyar). This was part of a Calonarang performance being done by ASTI as a *tari lepas* in 1969. The dance was modified by I Wayan Beratha in 1972 into its present form. Movements were taken from the traditional Rejang dance. Young women carrying bowls with burning incense dance in pairs, wafting the smoke towards the heavens, and at the end tossing the flower petals to the audience. A few years later, in 1972, Beratha created "Panyembrama" with simpler movements than "Gabor." Along with "Pendet" (not to be confused with the improvised, sacred Mendet), they are now the first dances learned by young girls. No headdresses are worn. In all of these dances, there is a prayer sequence and flower petals are scattered.

A much newer version of the welcome dance is "Puspawresti" (Showering Flowers), choreographed by I Wayan Dibia in 1981 with music by I Nyoman Windha for the opening of a newly paved road. The young female dancers carry bowls of flowers and are flanked by rows of young male dancers carrying spears. This is done to welcome special guests and was

inspired by the ceremonial Baris and Rejang dances.

"Sekar Jagat" (Flower of the World, another word for woman) was choreographed by Ni Luh Swasthi Wijaya in 1993. Taking movements from Rejang in Asak, this dance is distinctive for its elaborate headdress and *cane* (cha-nay) offering carried in the dancer's hands. The music was composed by I Nyoman Windha and is based on the *selonding* music of Tenganan Pegeringsingan village.

New Warriors

As part of the obligatory pieces for the Gong Kebyar Festival in 1979, I Nyoman Catra choreographed "Baris Bandana Manggala Yudha." This is a group Baris dance performed by young boys, depicting warriors of the King of Badung preparing for battle against the Dutch. The heroic scenes of this dance appear at the end where dancers draws daggers and fight. The music was composed by I Komang Astita.

"Wira Yudha," created in 1979 by I Wayan Dibia, is based on the ceremonial Baris Tumbak. A group of paired male dancers, each carrying a lance, utilizes movements from the martial arts and combat. The distinctive cloth headdress (*udeng*) differentiates this from other Baris dances.

"Satya Brastha" depicts a great fight between Prince Gatotkaca of the Pandawa and Karna of the Korawa in the "Bharata Yudha" battle. Gatotkaca is killed by Karna. The climax of this dance is the clever portrayal of a chariot using umbrellas and oversized dance fans with some of the dancers as horses. This was choreographed by I Nyoman Cerita in 1986 with music by I Nyoman Pasek.

The Arrival of Animals

Animal dances have become quite popular since the 1960s. Innovations in costuming and exaggerated movements on the part of the animals produce dances which are well-loved by local and international audiences alike.

The first of this type is the "Frog Dance," for which the village of Batuan is well known. In the 1930s, I Made Nurada created the Gamelan Genggong with comic rhythmic movements imitating the catching of frogs. The late I Nyoman Kakul conceived of using a tale from the *Panji* cycle later on in the l950s. The prince of Daha was hunting in the forest. He urinated in a coconut, which was found by a woman who then drank it. She became pregnant and gave birth to a frog. He grew up and wanted to marry the king's daughter. His mother was too embarrassed to go to the palace to ask for the princess's hand, but she finally relented. Three times she went to see the king and each time she was killed. But her son the frog brought her back to life. The frog married the beautiful princess, but he was so unhappy that he was ugly, he meditated and asked to be changed into a handsome prince. Siwa (portrayed in the dance as Rangda) appears and grants his wish.

"Kelinci," choreographed by I Nyoman Cerita in 1987, is a dance about rabbits performed by young girls. The basic *agem* position of Balinese dance is still inherent in these animal dances.

Combing Different Cultural Elements

In the 1980s, a plethora of bird dances appeared on the scene, many of them excerpts from Sendratari. "Manuk Rawa," created in 1982 by I Wayan Dibia with music by I Wayan Beratha, depicts a flock of waterbirds frolicking in a tranquil forest lake. In the original Bale Gala-Gala drama, the birds were showing Bima, who had just escaped from a burning house, where to find water. Movements include traditional Balinese, those from a West Javanese peacock dance as well as ballet. This piece was the inspiration for later bird dances.

"Belibis" (Wild Ducks) was created in 1984 by Swasthi Wijaya with music by Nyoman Windha as part of the Sendratari Angling Dharma. A new style of costume appears: long flowing skirts made out of blue strips of cloth, white satin wings and caps of white feathers. The dance depicts a flock of wild ducks, one of which is the transformation of Angling Dharma (a king who has been cursed by witches). This dance is a favorite among young women dancers.

Another work by the same team is "Cendrawasih," a dance depicting birds of paradise. This duet

Above: An example of one of ISI's final examination pieces, using elaborate costuming and stage props.

Below: I Nyoman Sura and I Wayan Darsana in "Tajen" (cockfight). One of the ARTI Foundation's signature pieces, this metaphorically depicts conflict in society through a cockfight.

This *kreasi baru*, "Giri Putri," was choreographed in 2003 by Ida Ayu Wimba with music by I Ketut Garwa. Elements of Wayang Kulit, as seen in the modern Tree of Life puppets (*kayonan*), are integrated into the dance.

"Nebuk Padi," performed in Pengosekan, is a dance where young girls portray village life by pounding rice.

Under the supervision of I Made Sidia, five *dalang* combine their skills with powerpoint projections in a new type of "wayang on skateboards" for children traumatized by the Kuta bomb blast.

was choreographed in 1988. Two young women act as a female bird and her male mate. They tease one another by showing off their colorful feathers. The long pink and white skirts and the Panji-like headdresses, crescent shaped with two long feathers, are distinctive of this dance.

Combining movements from Bali and Java is "Jaran Teji", a dance depicting Princess Sekar Teji and her servants who disguise themselves as horse riders, carrying shields and riding whips. Inspired by Sanghyang Jaran, both the music and the dance were created by I Wayan Dibia in 1985.

"Kijang Kencana" (Golden Deer) shows deer running through the forest. It is usually danced by young girls wearing antlers and bright yellow blouses and pants. Their exuberance and playfulness come through quite strongly as they leap like deer. This dance was inspired by the same figures found in the Javanese Sendratari Ramayana. It was created by I Gusti Agung Ngurah Supartha in 1983.

"Kembang Kirang" was inspired by Joged, Janger and Jaipongan from West Java. It was produced by the Werdhi Budaya Art Centre. Five young women strut their stuff on stage, flinging their sashes and smiling coquettishly.

"Nritta Dewi," also called "Chandra Wulan," is inspired by the South Indian classical dance Bharatanatyam and elongated Balinese paintings. This sensual dance of welcome was created by Ni Kadek Dewi Aryani for her final examination at STSI in 2001 and is now done at the Lotus Cafe performances in Ubud.

New Works with New Approaches

Bali's young choreographers and composers are primarily graduates from KOKAR/SMKI and ASTI/ISI, which both teach modern choreographic concepts. In a few other villages, modern dance (or a "conception" of what this is) has influenced staging, costume and movement. In Peliatan, for example, A. A. Gede Oka Dalem has been tremendously influenced by the works of Guruh Soekarnoputra (the first president Soekarno's son and a well-known choreographer). His group PANAS puts on frequent shows of Oka Dalem's latest works. The ARTI Foundation in Denpasar, run by I Kadek Suardana, uses more traditional forms and puts a new twist on them, as in "Gambuh Macbeth."

"Legong Untung Surapati," choreographed by

Guruh Soekarnoputra with music by I Gusti Kompiang Raka in 1995, combines elements of traditional Balinese dance, ballroom dancing, drum bands and themes of Dutch colonialism.

"Nebuk Padi" was choreographed by I Wayan Purwanto for the Bali Arts Festival in 1997. Performed by a number of young girls and boys, this piece depicts the pounding and the winnowing of rice. The girls' headdresses are distinctive.

"Legong Sunda-Upasunda" is a collossal 70-minute-long Legong dance performed by 20 young women depicting the tale of two brothers (Sunda-Upasunda, see p. 74) from the *Mahabharata*. It was choreographed in 1998 by I Wayan Dibia with music by I Made Arnawa.

The preceding dances have a number of modern elements, as seen in the musical accompaniment, costuming and, of course, movements. But the main influence is still from traditional Balinese dance. There are a number of much more contemporary forms.

"Cak Rina" may be considered to be the forerunner of contemporary dance in Bali. First performed in Teges Kanginan (Peliatan, Gianyar) by the Indonesian choreographer Sardono W. Kusuma in 1972, this dance has always been the center of controversy. Sardono and a number of young artists from the Taman Ismail Marzuki Art Centre in Jakarta came to Bali and decided to use the story of the monkey brothers Subali and Sugriwa in a Cak performance. Instead of incorporating the central lamp tree of traditional Kecak, many of the actors carry *obor-obor* (kerosene torches). Very young boys also hold torches and at that time a few of them were stark naked, which the local community found difficult to accept. Today, Sardono's version has been revised by I Ketut Rina (one of the original young boys in the 1970s) and is done at the ARMA Museum twice a month.

Other Forms of Cak

In l976, I Wayan Dibia created "Cak Subali-Sugriwa" based on an episode from the *Ramayana*. The Cak begins with the god Indra descending to where Subali and Sugriwa are meditating to ask for their help to kill the buffalo demons.

In the piece, the performers make all kinds of configurations, such as a cave, rocks upon which the monkeys are meditating and trees. Unlike the traditional Kecak where the chorus mainly sits, here the performers are very active, rolling around and running all over the stage, dancing in slow motion as well as in "fast-forward," and laughing and shouting. As with the Sardono Cak, *obor-obor* replace the tree of oil lamps. Subali and Sugriwa fight on the shoulders of their fellow actors. At the end, Subali is wrapped in a white shroud and carried offstage.

Dibia has also staged another type of Kecak at Kuta beach at sunset. Following the plot of the *Mahabharata* story "Dewi Ruci," in which Bima searches for holy water under the sea, the Cak performers cavort in the waves. Dibia's Cak always involves hundreds of performers; one such show in Nusa Dua in 1998 had 1,000 choral members!

Influence of the Bali Arts Festival

Gong Kebyar competitions held at the Bali Arts Festival (Pesta Kesenian Bali or PKB) have had a significant impact on the development of the performing arts. This is due to the fact that each participating group must present a new piece based on traditional forms. SMKI and ISI each produce a Sendratari for the PKB, and excerpts from these can become independent dances. Moreover, the final exams of ISI students require the creation of an original piece by individual students. Some *kreasi baru* become so popular that they are integrated into the repertoire performed at secular and religious venues.

Contemporary Polemics

Stemming from I Wayan Dibia's final exam piece at ASTI Yogyakarta in 1974, "Setan Bercanda" depicts a group of demons dancing in the middle of the night and spreading disease. When it was shown on local television in 1978, it created quite a polemic in the papers and among the literati. Many people felt that Dibia's unusual and challenging dance vocabulary threatened what they regarded as traditional dance values. His reputation as a controversial, even wacky, choreographer began here, and new performance pieces went through a period of hiatus after this.

"Gambuh Macbeth" was created in 1997 by I Kadek Suardana and members of the ARTI Foundation in Denpasar. Retaining the integrity and formality of Gambuh, they changed the storyline and costumes to produce a more "British" flavor.

"Ram-wana" (When Rama Becomes Rawana) was a colossal production integrating poetry, singing, shadow puppetry, dance and gamelan for the commemoration of I Wayan Dibia's professorship at STSI in 1999. The theme of the good king Rama transforming into the malicious and greedy Rawana reflected the political situation at that time.

"Wayang Dasa Nama Kerta" was created as a response to the Kuta bomb blast of 2002. Using a very large screen and LCD projections, *dalang* I Made Sidia initiated a wayang performance using the theme of overcoming the demons that are within us. This was taken into schools and villages with a psychiatrist to assist in the post-bomb trauma counseling. In this work, Sidia developed a new technique of playing the puppets using skateboards and multiple *dalang* (see www.ykip.org for details).

I Nyoman Sura and I Nengah Darsana in a love scene between Lady Macbeth and her husband in "Gambuh Macbeth."

Young children always play the role of small frogs in the "Frog Dance" with carefree and joyful movements.

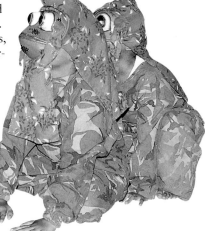

New Music

Since the 1970s, many new types of gamelan and fusion music have emerged in Bali. Most musicians continue to use traditional instruments but are either playing new types of music on them or using them in unusual ways. Others are developing totally new kinds of gamelan. Musical compositions are influenced by music from all over Indonesia as well as from other parts of the world. Collaborations are now a common occurrence at the Bali Arts Festival.

Adi Mredangga, a marching gamelan, features extra large drums and cymbals played by numerous musicians. The marching sequences are highly stylized. Adi Mredangga usually opens the Bali Arts Festival parade.

Chandra Wira Buana, Semaradhana, Ubud. One of the few places one can hear the Semaradhana gamelan is at the Lotus Pond Stage in Ubud. This versatile gamelan can play in both the five- and seven-tone scales.

Contemporary music in Bali can be placed in two categories: those innovations that introduce new musical ideas and concepts into the traditional gamelan, and those that create new instruments to build a new type of ensemble. The first development includes the use of new rhythmic patterns or works which transform ritual, social and political activities into the sound of music. The second involves expanding or changing the traditional gamelan orchestra to create a new type of ensemble.

New Music on Traditional Gamelan

New types of music played on traditional gamelan includes works for Kebyar compositions, Sendratari, and totally new forms of music.

In 1968, during the Mredangga Utsava Festival Gong Kebyar (the first of the annual arts festivals), new compositions were heard in the *lelambatan* and *kebyar* styles. In this, new rhythmic structures of three, five and seven beats (instead of the normal four and eight) were used. In the 1970s, with the advent of Sendratari, performed on a large proscenium stage with the actors at a distance from the audi-ence, a louder sound was needed. The Gamelan Geguntangan was expanded to include a number of *kulkul* (wooden gongs), *gong pulu* (iron gongs) and the original *curing* (iron metallophones). In 1973, at ASTI/ISI, it became a graduation requirement that each student produce a *kreasi baru* (new creation) in music, dance or puppetry.

The 1970s and 1980s were a time of change in the music world. A lot of experimental work rooted in tradition emerged. Some composers transformed religious ceremonies into music, such as I Komang Astita in 1979 with his "Gema Dasa Rudra" (depicting the 100-year ritual of Eka Dasa Rudra), the first time that both *pelog* and *slendro* scales were played in the same ensemble, and "Kosong" by I Ketut Gede Asnawa in 1984, a musical dramatization of the procession of the cleansing of the gods before Nyepi, the Balinese Day of Silence. Asnawa tried to evoke the essence of silence through non-musical objects, such as plastic bags, palm-rib brooms and stones.

Adi ("best, foremost") Mredangga ("drum") was created in 1984 by STSI/ISI and performed at the Bali Arts Festival that year. This is a large marching ensemble based on Balaganjur, featuring a great number of drums and gongs. Unlike Balaganjur, Adi Mredangga has a strong sense of dance to it, whereby the musicians' movements are choreographed. There can be up to 150 performers.

In 1985, Gentara Pinara Pitu developed out of the seven-note *pelog* Gamelan Semar Pagulingan, the main difference being that the *gangsa* (metallophones) now span two octaves instead of one. This was the brainchild of I Wayan Beratha, the well-known musician and maker of gamelan. He wanted to be able to play both Kebyar and Semar Pagulingan style music in one ensemble. Because Gentara Pinara Pitu is difficult to play, this style has never attained great popularity.

Semaradhana (Semara is the god of love and *dhana* means "generous," the name given in the hope that there would be a little something for everyone) also developed out of the seven-note *pelog* Gamelan Semar Pagulingan. In 1988, I Wayan Beratha tried once again to make a combination gamelan, this time with more success. Even though this new gamelan ensemble is difficult to play, as both the *pelog* and *slendro* scales are on all the metallophones, musicians find it more versatile.

Other compositions expressed the atmosphere of daily activities in the rice field, such as "Uma Sadina," also composed by Astita in 1982. Other works turned to the political situation of Indonesia, such as the spirit of "unity in diversity" and transformed it into a musical composition. "Sumpah Palapa" was composed by I Nyoman Windha using three different sets of gamelan: Gamelan Semar Pagulingan, Gong Gede and some Javanese gamelan instruments.

"Body Tjak" combines Body Music and *cak* (vocal chant) and is the result of a long collaboration between the American percussionist Keith Terry and I Wayan Dibia. In 1990, the first experiments took place with 22 performers (11 Americans and 11 Indonesians), and in 1999 Body Tjak Celebration toured both Bali and California.

"Laya" by I Wayan Gede Yudana was first performed in 1991 for his STSI examinations. By playing Balinese drums like congas, using *rebab* bows to play the *gangsa* by bowing the sides of the keys and incorporating Tibetan bells and Western music, the musicians created a new kind of soundscape. This piece describes freedom in a variety of rhythms of life.

In 1991, Bajra Sandhi fused the sounds of Semar Pagulingan, Gong Gede and Gamelan Selonding to produce their unique sound.

An innovative group from Pengosekan, Çudamani, under the directorship of Dewa Putu Beratha, has utilized the versatility of Gamelan Semaradhana to create new compositions and collaborations with artists from all over the world. Wayang Listrik (see p. 49) is one of their signature pieces.

Gamelan Sekar Jaya (Flowering Victory) of California has made the performing arts of Bali its specialty. The group's success arises not only from its devotion to a traditional repertoire but from its innovative work. Since its inception in 1979, it has sponsored the creation of more than fifty major new works for gamelan and dance. They have helped in inspiring the young people of Bali to continue to learn about their traditional art forms as well as to show women that they, too, can be musicians. During the group's most recent tour to Bali, in June 2000, it received a Dharma Kusuma award, Bali's highest award for artistic achievement, never before given to foreign performers.

New Music with New Gamelan

Gamelan Maniksanti (*manik* means "jewel" and *santi* "peace") is a recent innovation, created by I Wayan Sinti in 1994. It resembles a Gamelan Pelegongan or Gamelan Semar Pagulingan but each instrument has fourteen notes, so it is extremely versatile. Music can be played from a variety of repertoires. It is found only in Ubung Kaja in Denpasar.

Gamelan Genggong is mostly performed at tourist venues as the "Frog Dance." This relatively obscure form is named for its *genggong* ("jew's harp") made out of the main stalks of the sugar palm tree. The songs played in the *slendro* scale are reminiscent of farmers' songs. Trying to get the music to sound right is not an easy feat: the split "tongue" of the instrument vibrates between the lips by tugging a string on the right end. Notes are achieved by inhaling and exhaling; and by changing the shape of the mouth. The resulting sounds are like those made by frogs.

Contemporary Works

I Gusti Ngurah Adiputra in Bona Kelod, Gianyar, has been attracted to the music of other cultures for many years. After spending time in Hong Kong, he made an *erhu* (Chinese bowed lute) which he uses to perform with the Sanggar Bona Alit Gamelan Semar Pagulingan. Two electric guitars and palm rib brooms struck against the palm of the hand add their own flavor to this combination of rock and gamelan music. Adiputra has succeeded in mimicking keyboard effects by using natural materials and sounds, including having live crickets perform on cue! The ensemble plays not only traditional music, but also popular songs such as the theme song from "Titanic." Another example is Batuan Ethnik Fusion led by I Wayan Balawan, combining jazz music with Balinese gamelan. They can be heard every Tuesday night at the Jazz Cafe in Tebesaya, Peliatan.

I Wayan Dibia and American percussionist Keith Terry combining the rhythms of *cak* and Body Music in "Body Tjak," 1990.

Gamelan Sekar Jaya performing at Noe Valley Ministry, San Francisco, in the late 1990s. Guest music director, I Made Subandi, plays the drum at center.

A Hundred Years of Balinese Dance, Theater and Music

1900s Joged Pingitan, a dance using the *Calonarang* story, created.

1914 Arja Doyong, a form of sung dance-drama, appeared on the streets.

1910 Kebyar Legong, the first form of *bebancihan* (cross-dressing) dance, created by I Wayan Wandres of Jagaraja, North Bali.

1915 Gamelan Gong Kebyar created in North Bali. Mebarung, also known as the "battle of the bands," began.

1920s Women started taking on female and refined male roles in Arja.

1925 Kebyar Duduk, a dance performed while seated, created by I Ketut Maria (Mario).

1928 First performance of the Condong or maidservant in Legong by I Wayan Rindi.

Late 1920s Janger, a form of dance utilizing call and response singing, created.

1930 Kecak Ramayana created by I Wayan Limbak and Walter Spies in Bedulu.

1930s Classical Legong renamed Legong Keraton. Emergence of *tari lepas* or non-dramatic dances.

1931 Sekaa Gong Peliatan performed at the World Colonial Exposition in Paris.

Early 1940s Palawakia, where the dancer both sings and plays the *trompong*, created.

1942 Prembon dance-drama (a fusion of Arja and Topeng styles) appeared. "Margapati" and "Demang Miring," both *bebancihan* dances, created by I Nyoman Kaler.

1943 "Panji Semirang," a *bebancihan* dance, created by I Nyoman Kaler and I Wayan Lotring.

1945 Republic of Indonesia gained its independence. "Wiranata" dance created by I Nyoman Ridet.

1952 Sekaa Gong Peliatan performed on Broadway, New York. "Oleg Tambuliling-an"(Bumbleebee Dance) created by I Ketut Maria. Solo form of Taruna Jaya choreographed by I Gede Manik.

1957 "Tenun" (Weaving Dance) created by I Nyoman Ridet and I Wayan Likes.

1960 Konservatori Karawitan Indonesia (KOKAR) or High School of Balinese Performing Arts, established in Denpasar.

First Sendratari (Jayaprana) created by I Wayan Beratha at KOKAR.

1965 Sendratari Ramayana, first Ramayana Ballet, created by I Wayan Beratha at KOKAR. Communist coup occurred, resulting in the deaths of numerous Balinese performing artists.

1966 Drama Gong, the Balinese vernacular drama, created by A. A. Raka Payadnya.

1967 Akademi Seni Tari Indonesia (ASTI) or Indonesian Academy of Dance, now Institute of Indonesian Arts (ISI), formed.

1968 First all-Bali Gong Kebyar Competition held in Denpasar.

1970 "Gabor," first welcome dance, created by I Gusti Gede Raka of Saka.

1971 Majelis Pertimbangan dan Pembinaan Kebudayaan (LISTIBIYA) or Bali Arts Council, hosted Regional Seminar of Sacred and Profane Arts.

1972 "Panyembrama" offering dance created by I Wayan Beratha. "Kecak Rina" created by Sardono W. Kusuma at Banjar Teges Kanginan, Gianyar. "Kecak Dasarath Gugur" created by I Wayan Dibia at Singapadu, Gianyar.

1975 Taman Werdhi Budaya (Bali Art Centre), the largest in Indonesia, opened in Denpasar. Wayang Arja created by I Made Sija of Bona, Gianyar.

1978 Televisi Republik Indonesia (TVRI) began operations in Denpasar. "Setan Bercanda" created by I Wayan Dibia.

1979 Pesta Kesenian Bali (PKB) or annual Bali Arts Festival began. "Bina Tari," a television show teaching Balinese dance, started by Ni Ketut Arini Alit.

1980 First women's gamelan group started by Ni Ketut Suryatini in Denpasar.

1981 Wayang Kulit Tantri started by I Made Persib of STSI Denpasar. This form later developed by I Wayan Wija.

1982 Bumbang, a new bamboo ensemble, created by I Nyoman Rembang of Denpasar. "Manukrawa," first of the bird dances, created by I Wayan Dibia.

1983 "Belibis" (Swan Dance) created by Ni Luh Nyoman Swasthi Wijaya and I Nyoman Windha.

1985 Gamelan Sekar Jaya of California, USA, participated in the annual Bali Arts Festival, the first time a foreign gamelan group had been asked to perform. First Festival Gong Wanita (Women's Gamelan Festival) held. Genta Pinara Pitu, a new seven-tone *pelog* gamelan, created by I Wayan Beratha.

1986 Gamelan Sekar Jepun of Tokyo, Japan, participated in the Bali Arts Festival.

1988 Gamelan Semaradhana, a new gamelan using both five and seven tones, created by I Wayan Beratha. "Rejang Dewa" dance created by NLN Swasthi Bandem.

1989 Wayang Lebar (large screen shadow puppet show) created by I Ketut Kodi.

Early 1990s Arja Muani, an all-male Arja troupe began performing.

1990–91 Festival of Indonesia held in the US, featuring Kecak and Legong from Bali.

1990 "Body Tjak" created by Keith Terry and I Wayan Dibia in northern California.

1992 Children's gamelan groups began participating in the Bali Arts Festival.

1994 Gamelan Manikasanti created by I Wayan Sinti of Ubung village, Denpasar.

1996 First Nusa Dua Arts Festival held, now an annual event. Wayang Listrik (Electric Wayang using a wide screen) created by Larry Reed, premiered at Walter Spies Festival.

1997 "Gambuh Macbeth" created by I Kadek Suardana and ARTI Foundation.

1998 Merajut Tali Keberagaman Karawitan Bali, a concert using nine sets of gamelan, produced by STSI.

2000 "Nyurya Sewana" created by I Wayan Dibia and Kadek Suardana to greet the new millennium.

2002 Wayang Dasa Nama Kerta (wayang on skateboards) created by Made Sidia after the Bali bombing of October 12, 2002). New television station, BALI TV, opened.

2003 First Indonesian Performing Arts Mart (IPAM) held in Bali.

2004 STSI became ISI.

Resource Guide

Below is an abbreviated list of where you can see Balinese performing arts as well as where to find things such as instruments, puppets, masks and dance costumes.

There are hundreds of troupes on the island, so this list is by no means exhaustive. There are particular companies or dancers who are well known for a particular style or role and you can catch them at a festival or other ritual. Your hotel or local tourist board may be able to give you information about special performances. Check out the Taman Budaya Art Centre and ISI in Denpasar as well as the local tourist publications. The Bali-oriented websites sometimes have information on local performances as well.

In the Ubud area, the programs set up for tourists remain fairly set, but due to dancers' availability sometimes substitutions will occur. If there is a particular dance that you want to see, then you can check their program.

CLASSES

ARMA (Agung Rai Museum of Art), Jalan Bima, Pengosekan, Ubud. Tel: 0361/976659; Fax: 0361/973495; E-mail: armaubud@denpasar.wasantara.net.id; www.nusantara.com/arma/. Children's gamelan and dance classes

ARTI Foundation (Kadek Suardana), Werdhi Budaya Art Centre, Jalan Nusa Indah, Denpasar. Tel: 0361/236619

Bajra Sandhi (Ida Wayan Oka Granoka), Jalan Kebo Iwa, Banjar Batukandik, Denpasar. Tel: 0361/412203

Çudamani (Dewa Putu Beratha and Emiko Mitoma Susilo), Jalan Raya, Pengosekan, Ubud. Tel: 0361/977067 or 972533; E-mail: cudamani@indo.net.id

ISI (Institut Seni Indonesia/Indonesian Institute of the Arts), Jalan Nusa Indah, Denpasar. Tel: 0361/227316; Fax: 0361/233100

SMKI (Sekolah Menengah Karawitan Indonesia/Indonesian High School of Performing Arts), Batubulan, Gianyar. Tel: 0361/298163

WARINI (Ni Ketut Arini Alit), Jalan Kecubung, Gang Soka I, Banjar Lebah, Denpasar. Tel/Fax: 0361/228644; E-mail: warini@dps.centrin.net.id. Children's dance classes: Tues., Thurs., Sat. afternoons & Sun. mornings

Yayasan Polosseni, Teges Kanginan, Peliatan, Ubud. Tel: 0361/975869. E-mail: polos@goarchi.com.; www.goarchi.com/yp/. Gamelan and dance classes.

COSTUMES

Kios Sri Gati (all types of dance ornaments and costumes), South of the Art Market, Jalan Raya, Sukawati. Tel: 0361/299146

Printing Mas Studio (dance costumes), Jalan Meduri No. 11A, Banjar Abian Kapas Kaja, Denpasar. Tel: 0361/232826. Hours: 9 a.m.–4 p.m. Mon–Sat.

I Made Reda (leather ornaments), Banjar Puaya, Sukawati. Tel: 0361/299476

MASK-MAKERS

Cokorda Raka Tisnu (barong), Puri Saren Kangin, Singapadu. Tel: 0361/298671

Ida Bagus Alit (traditional), Jalan Raya Lod Tunduh, Lod Tunduh, Ubud. Tel: 0361/977537

Ida Bagus Anom (traditional and contemporary), Jalan Raya Mas, Mas, Gianyar. Tel/Fax: 0361/975292

I Nyoman Setiawan and **I Made Regug** (traditional), Banjar Lantang Idung, Batuan. Tel: 0361/294528; E-mail: nysetiawan@yahoo.com

I Wayan Tangguh (traditional), Banjar Mukti, Singapadu. Tel: 0361/298685

PUPPET MAKERS AND PUPPETEERS

I Wayan Mardika, Banjar Babakan, Sukawati. Tel: 0361/299646

I Wayan Nartha, Banjar Babakan, Sukawati. Tel: 0361/299080; E-mail: wira@ekawidabali.com

I Wayan Wija, Banjar Kalah, Peliatan, Ubud. Tel: 0361/973367; antonwija@hotmail.com

CDS, CASSETTES AND VCDS

Ganesha Books, Jalan Raya Ubud, Ubud. Tel: 0361/970320; Fax: 0361/973359; E-mail: info@ganeshbooksbali.com; www.ganeshabooksbali.com

Nova Music, Jalan Cokorda Rai Budak (Jalan Raya), Peliatan, Ubud. Tel: 0361/974862

Toko Melati, Jalan Kartini No. 31, Denpasar. Tel: 0361/222092

INSTRUMENTS

Moira Music Shop, Jalan Raya Ubud No. 4, Ubud. Tel: 0361/977367; E-mail: moari_bali@yahoo.com; www.bali 3000.com/moari

Sidhakarya Gong Foundry, Banjar Babakan, Blahbatuh, Gianyar. Tel/Fax: 0361/942798

Genggong: I Wayan Pageh, Br Geleka, Batuan

Kendang: I Rudita, Gulingan, Kapal; I Made Sukerta, Br Babekan, Blahbatuh; I Wayan Sadra, Pindha, Blahbatuh

Suling bambu: Cokorda Bagus Wiranata, Jalan Cok. Rai Budak, Peliatan. Tel: 0361/975134; I Wayan Sadra, Pindha, Blahbatuh

Suling Gambuh: I Wayan Roja, Br Geleka, Batuan

Tingklik, I Made Terip, Munduk, Buleleng; I Wayan Muda, Pengosekan, Ubud.

PERFORMANCES in Gianyar Regency
(Tickets average Rp 50,000)

Anangga Sari Troupe: Legong Dance
(Thurs. 7.30–9 p.m.), Banjar Kelod, Kutuh,
Ubud. *Sekar Sari (inst.), Gabor, Rabbit Dance,
Legong Lasem, Anangga Sari Winangung
(inst.), Kebyar Duduk* or *Cendrawasih* or
Topeng Tua, Oleg Tambulilingan

Barong Den Jalan (Daily 9.30–10.30 a.m.),
Batubulan

Bina Remaja: Legong Dance (Sat. 7.30–8.50
p.m.), Ubud Palace, Jalan Raya, Ubud. *Kebyar
Dang (inst.), Puspa Wresti, Topeng Keras,
Legong Keraton Lasem, Kebyar Duduk, Kupu-
Kupu Tarum, Oleg Tambulilingan, Jauk*

Cak Rina Dance (every full and dark moon
7.00–8.10 p.m.), ARMA Museum, Jalan Bima,
Peliatan. Tel: 0361/976659; info@armamuse-
um.com. Latest creation of *Kecak* by I Wayan
Rina of Teges Kangingan

Chandra Wati Women's Gamelan with child
dancers (Tues. 7.30–9.00 p.m.), behind the
Lotus Cafe, Jalan Raya, Ubud. *Inst., Crukcuk
Punyah, Pusa Wresti, Cendrawasih, Panji
Semirang, Rabbit Dance, Topeng Monyet*

Chandra Wira Buana (Sat. 7.30–9.00 p.m.),
behind the Lotus Cafe, Jalan Raya, Ubud.
*Candra Wulan, Kebyar Trompong, Legong
Semaradhana, Topeng Tua, Satya Brasta*

Gambuh Desa Adat Batuan (every 1st and 15th
of the month, 7–9 p.m.), Pura Desa, Batuan

Genta Bhuana Sari (Tues. 7.30–8.40 p.m.),
Balerung Mandera Srinertya Waditra Stage,
Banjar Teruna, Peliatan, Ubud. Tel: 0361/
972124; Fax: 0361/970503. *Sekar Jepun (inst.),
Puspa Sari* or *Pendet, Baris Tunggal, Legong
Lasem, Kelinci, Gambang Suling (inst.), Cen-
drawasih, Jauk* or *Topeng*

Gong Kebyar Gunung Sari Peliatan (Sat.
7.30–9.00 p.m.), Wantilan Pura Dalem
Puri. *Inst., Gabor* or *Pendet, Baris, Kebyar
Trompong, Legong Keraton Lasem, Gambang
Suling (inst.), Oleg Tambulilingan, Topeng,
Barong*

Jaya Suara: Legong of Mahabrata (Sun. 7.30–
8.30 p.m.), Ubud Palace, Jalan Raya, Ubud

Kecak and Fire Dance (Mon. 7.00–8.00 p.m.),
Junjungan village (transportation at UTI)

Kecak Banjar Tengah, Peliatan (Thurs.
7.30–8.15 p.m.), Puri Agung Peliatan, Ubud

**Krama Desa Adat Ubud Kaja: Kecak, Fire and
Trance Dance** (Mon. & Fri. 7.30–8.30 p.m.),
Jaba Pura Dalem Ubud, Jalan Raya, Ubud

Panca Arta: Legong Dance (Wed. 7.30–9.00
p.m.), Ubud Palace, Jalan Raya, Ubud. *Overture
(inst), Legong Keraton Lasem, Barong, Sunda
Upasunda drama*

Panca Arta: Gabor Dance (Thurs. 7.30–9.00
p.m.), Ubud Palace, Jalan Raya, Ubud. *Kebyar
Trompong* or *Kebyar Duduk, Kijang Kencana,
Topeng Tua* or *Jauk, The Ballet of Abimanyu*

Peliatan Masters/Seke Werdha ARMA (Sun.
7.30 p.m. except new and full moons), ARMA
Museum, Jalan Bima, Peliatan. Tel: 0361/
976659; info@armamuseum.com. *Pendet,
Legong Lasem, Oleg Tambulilingan, Taruna
Jaya* or *Cock-fighting Dance, Baris* and
Semaradhana gamelan demonstration

Raja Peni: Barong and Keris Dance (Thurs.
7.30–9.00 p.m.), Pura Dalem, Ubud

Sadha Budaya Troupe: Barong Dance (Fri.
7.00–8.10 p.m.), Ubud Palace, Jalan Raya,
Ubud. *Barong solo, Calonarang story*

Sadha Budaya Troupe: Legong Dance (Mon.
7.30–9.00 p.m.), Ubud Palace, Jalan Raya,
Ubud. *Inst., Gabor, Baris, Legong Keraton
Lasem, Kindama (inst.), Taruna Jaya, Oleg
Tambulilingan, Topeng Tua, Inst.*

Sandhi Suara Troupe: Barong and Kris Dance
(Mon. 7.00–8.10 p.m.), Jaba Pura Padang

Kerta, Padang Tegal Kelod, Ubud. *Welcome
dance, Barong, Sunda Upasunda*

**Sandhi Suara Troupe: Kecak, Fire and Trance
Dance** (Tues. & Thurs. 7.30–8.30 p.m.), Jaba
Pura Padang Kerta, Padang Tegal Kelod, Ubud

Sanggar ARMA Kumara Sari: Satya Brasta
(Children's dance and gamelan, Sat. 7.30–8.30
p.m.), ARMA Museum, Jalan Bima, Peliatan.
Tel: 0361/976659; info@armamuseum.com.
*Pendet, Legong Lasem, Inst., Baris, Kreasi Baru
Nebuk Padi, Satya Brasta*

Semara Pagulingan TIRTA SARI (Fri. 7.30–
8.50 p.m.), Balerung Mandera Srinertya
Waditra Stage, Banjar Teruna, Peliatan, Ubud.
Tel: 0361/972124; Fax: 0361/970503. *Sekar
Gendot (inst.), Puspa Mekar, Legong Lasem,
Kebyar Trompong/Duduk, Legong Jobog* or
Legong Kuntir or *Taruna Jaya* or *Oleg Tambu-
lilingan* or *Baris, Barong Tarupramana* or *Telek*

Semara Ratih Troupe: Spirit of Bali (Tues.
7.30–9 p.m.), Banjar Kelod, Kutuh, Ubud.
Tel/Fax: 0361/973277. Program changes weekly
but includes *Baris, Legong Abimanyu, Barong,
Legong Kuntir, Legong Jobog, Legong Lasem,
Taruna Jaya, Palawakia, Barong Ket, Telek,
Ramayana Ballet fragment).* Seniman Tua (old
master dancers) on last Tuesday of month

Shadow Puppet Play "Calonarang" (Tues. &
Sat. 8–9.15 p.m.), Kerta Accommodations,
Jalan Monkey Forest, Ubud

Shadow Puppet Play "Mahabharata" excerpt
(Sun. & Wed. 8–9.15 p.m.), Oka Kartini
Hotel, Jalan Raya, Ubud. Tel: 0361/975193;
Fax: 0361 975759

Suara Sakti: Jegog Bamboo Gamelan (Sun.
7 p.m.), Bentuyung village

Trene Jenggala: Kecak Fire and Trance Dance
(Wed., Sat. & Sun. 7–8 p.m.), Padang Tegal,
Ubud

Yowana Swara: Jegog Bamboo Gamelan
(Wed. 7–8 p.m.), Pura Dalem, Ubud

Select Glossary

agem basic dance posture with weight on the back leg

alus refined, smooth, usually referring to a character type

angsel strong dance or musical accent, used to cue a change

Arja form of sung dance-drama

ASTI Akademi Seni Tari Indonesia (Indonesian Academy of Dance), now known as ISI

balih-balihan term used for dances done for entertainment

Baris solo male warrior dance

Baris Gede ritual warrior dance done by large groups of men

Barong Landung pair of larger-than-life body puppets, one male and one female

Barong sacred masked dance performed by two men; most usual form is Barong Ket (lion)

bebali semi-ceremonial dances of the middle courtyard, which supplement a ritual but are not the ritual themselves

bondres comic half-masked characters usually found in Topeng dance-drama

cak sound made by the male Kecak chorus in Sanghyang rituals and Kecak dance

Cakepung form of "mouth music" in which young men sit in a circle and sing

Calonarang dance-drama depicting the 11th century story of the widow-witch Rangda

ceng-ceng small set of cymbals, the bottom half mounted face up and the top half hand-held

ceng-ceng kopyak set of hand-held cymbals

colotomic phrase of music punctuated by different gongs

Condong maidservant

dalang puppeteer

Dalem the king in Topeng mask dance-drama

Delem in Wayang Kulit, younger brother of Sangut and on the "left" side

Drama Gong fusion of drama and gamelan, acted and spoken rather than danced

Gabor offering or welcome dance

Gambuh classical form of dance-drama said to be the basis of most dramatic forms and music in Bali

gamelan ensemble of mainly percussive instruments, including gongs, metallophones, drums, flutes, gong chimes and sometimes a lute

Gamelan Angklung four–or five-tone *slendro* ensemble performed at temple festivals and cremations

Gamelan Balaganjur marching gamelan using primarily cymbals, drums and inverted kettle gongs

Gamelan Caruk rare and ancient ensemble

Gamelan Gaguntangan ensemble of *guntang* or one-stringed bamboo zithers, flutes and drums which accompanies Arja

Gamelan Gambang sacred seven-tone *pelog* ensemble

Gamelan Gong Gede largest of the ensembles, tuned to *saih lima*

Gamelan Gong Kebyar the most prolific type of ensemble on the island today, played with many stops and starts

Gamelan Gong Luang sacred seven-tone *pelog* gamelan

Gamelan Jegog ensemble of giant bamboo instruments originating from West Bali

Gamelan Joged Bumbung set of bamboo xylophones which accompanies Joged flirtation dance

Gamelan Pelegongan five-tone *pelog* ensemble usually accompanying Legong dance

Gamelan Rindik bamboo ensemble used to accompany Joged dances

Gamelan Selonding seven-tone sacred gamelan made with iron keys

Gamelan Semar Pagulingan *saih pitu* court ensemble featuring the *trompong*

Gamelan Semaradhana new type of ensemble with extended keys so that both *pelog* and *slendro* scales can be played

Gandrung percursor to the Joged Bumbung flirtation dance in which dancers are male

gangsa generic term for a two-octave metallophone with resonators

gelungan leather tooled headdress

gender usually referring to metallophones played with two round-headed mallets

Gender Wayang set of four 10-keyed metallophones which accompany the Wayang Kulit

Genjek form of "mouth music" from East Bali

singing about daily life

grantang also called *tingklik* instruments made out of lashed bamboo tubes

ISI Institute Seni Indonesia (Indonesian Arts Institute), formerly ASTI (Akademi Seni Tari Indonesia or Indonesian Dance Academy) and STSI (Sekolah Tinggi Seni Indonesia or College of Indonesian Arts), Denpasar

Janger type of dance where young men and women use call and response songs

Jauk masked dance depicting a demon with long fingernails

jegogan "bass" *gangsa* metallophone of the gamelan

Joged Bumbung flirtation dance

jublag metallophone which plays core melody

kajar non-bossed kettle gong; the timekeeper

kalangan traditional stage space, surrounded by three sides

kasar coarse or rough, usually referring to a character type

Kawi form of Old or Middle Javanese language often used in classical dance-dramas and shadow puppet plays

kayonan or *kayon* Tree of Life in Wayang Kulit, symbolizing the world

Kebyar literally to "burst open." Refers to the style of music and dance which burst onto the scene in North Bali in 1915

Kebyar Duduk dance done by a solo male while seated on the ground

Kebyar Trompong dance done by a solo male who plays the *trompong*

Kecak refers to the male characters in the Janger dance as well as to the Kecak chorus whereby a large group of men chant *cak*

kemong small hanging gong which marks beat four; it alternates with the *kempur*

kempli small non-hanging gong

kempur medium-sized hanging gong which articulates the middle of a gong phrase

kendang two-headed drum

keras strong or coarse, usually referring to a style of dance or character

keris dagger worn by most male characters

klenang smallest of the non-hanging gongs which is played on the offbeat *klenteng* small, high-pitched hanging gong

KOKAR Konservatori Karawitan (Music Conservatory) now known as SMKI

kotekan interlocking parts, usually played on the *gangsa* metallophones

kreasi baru new creation, referring to the latest developments in the performing arts

lanang male; higher-pitched of a set of instruments

langse split dance curtain, demarcating the liminal space between dancer and audience

Legong Keraton dance performed by two girls originating in the early 18th century

lelambatan slow, stately type of gamelan music performed at temple ceremonies

madya lit. "middle," refers to the torso or middle section of a body, village, pillar; also refers to the post-Majapahit gamelan ensembles

Mahabharata Indian epic depicting the adventures of the five Pandawa brothers in exile and their 99 cousins, the Korawa

Majapahit East Javanese kingdom which flourished from 1343 to 1511 and greatly influenced Balinese culture

Mantri Buduh crazy prince or antagonist in Arja

Mantri Manis sweet prince or protagonist in Arja

mebarung "battle of the bands"

melaspas ritual in which objects such as masks are purified

Mendet type of dance done in the inner courtyard to welcome and send off the gods

Merdah in Wayang Kulit, son of Twalen and on the "right" side

metallophone xylophone with metal keys

mewinten ritual of purification for humans, undergone by dancers, actors, puppeteers

ngayah ritual devotion to the gods without expectation of remuneration

ngumbang ngisep musical term referring to the paired tuning of instruments

niskala unseen or psychic world

nista most unclean or polluted part of a body or village (most oceanward)

odalan temple anniversary, usually occuring every 210 days or every 12 months

Panasar Kelihan storyteller in Topeng dance-drama, older brother to Panasar Cenikan

panggul mallet used in playing instruments

Panji refined male character in Gambuh

Patih prime minister

pelog scale of uneven intervals, usually seven-tone but can be five-tone

Pendet form of temple dance done to welcome the gods; also a welcome dance

Pesta Kesenian Bali (PKB) annual Bali Arts Festival held mid-June to mid-July at the Werdhi Budaya Art Centre, Denpasar

pokok basic, foundation; refers to the core melody in music or the dance postures and walks which must be learned first

polos direct, simple; in music, one of two parts which most closely follows the melody (see *sangsih*)

pragina performer, actor-dancer

Prembon form of dance-drama featuring both characters of Topeng and Arja

Punakawan clown characters in Wayang Kulit

Putri princess character

Ramayana epic tale from India depicting the story of King Rama and Queen Sita, her abduction and subsequent rescue

Rangda Queen of Black Magic, this character plays a prominent role in many dance-dramas and in Wayang Calonarang

rangki the "green room" of theater or the backstage area behind the curtain

rebab two-stringed lute

Rejang sacred dance by groups of women

reyong set of twelve mounted inverted kettle gongs played by four musicians

saih lima five-tone scale derived from the seven-tone scale called *saih pitu* and used in Gamelans Gandrung, Gong Gede, Gong Kebyar and Pelegongan

saih pitu seven-tone scale used in Gamelans Gambang, Gambuh, Luang, Semar Pagulingan and Selonding

sanggar music or dance studio which also performs

Sanghyang form of trance-dance ritual

sangsih lit. "different"; in music, one of two parts which plays interlocking rhythms with the *polos* part

Sangut in Wayang Kulit, older brother of Delem and on the "left" side

saron type of xylophone which has only one large resonating chamber

sekaa club of musicians and/or dancers

sekala seen or conscious world

seledet darting eye movement which marks musical phrases

Sendratari form of pantomimed dance-drama started in the 1960s and still very popular among Balinese today

Sidhakarya lit. "he who finishes the work", the last mask performed in the Topeng Pajegan or solo ritual masked dance

sisya apprentices to Rangda, the witch, seen in the Calonarang dance-drama

slendro common five-tone scale similar to the pentatonic scale

SMKI Sekolah Menengah Karawitan Indonesia (Indonesian High School of Performing Arts), Batubulan

suling end-blown bamboo flute

taksu spiritual charisma of a performer

Tantri animal fables in the Wayang Kulit Tantri

tari lepas dances not attached to a drama; non-dramatic forms

Telek form of masked dance depicting deities

Topeng masked dance-drama in which the performers play multiple parts

Topeng Pajegan masked dance-drama in which one performer plays all the roles

Topeng Panca masked dance-drama with five actors playing all the roles

trompong set of ten mounted inverted kettle gongs played by one musician

Twalen in Wayang Kulit, father of Merdah and on the "right" side

ugal lead metallophone in a gamelan; also refers to the lead player who sits slightly higher than the other players

wadon female or lower-pitched instrument in a pair

wali lit. "offering"; refers to the most sacred types of dances performed in the inner courtyard of a temple

Wayang Kulit shadow puppet play in which puppets made from buffalo hide and representing characters from stories are cast upon a screen by a puppeteer

Wayang Lemah ritual form of shadow puppet theater performed with no screen

Wayang Wong form of dance-drama using masks and the *Ramayana* story

Select Bibliography (Works in English)

Bakan, Michael, *Music of Death and New Creation: Experiences in the World of Balinese Gamelan Beleganjur*, Chicago: University of Chicago Press, 1999.

Ballinger, Rucina, "Dance in Bali: The Passing on of a Tradition in Dance as Cultural Heritage," in Betty True Jones (ed.), *Dance as Cultural Heritage*, Vol. 2, Selected Papers from the ADG-CORD Conference, NY: Committee on Research in Dance, 1985.

Bandem, I Made, "The Baris Dance," *Ethnomusicology*, 19: 259–66, 1975.

_____, "The Barong Dance," *World of Music*, 18(3): 45–52, 1976.

_____, *Wayang Wong in Contemporary Bali*, Yogyakarta: Bali Mangsi Press, 2001.

Bandem, Made and Fredrik deBoer, "Gambuh: A Classical Balinese Dance Drama," *Asian Music*, 10(1): 115–27, 1978.

_____, *Kaja and Kelod: Balinese Dance in Transition*, 2nd edn, Kuala Lumpur: Oxford University Press, 1995.

Belo, Jane, *Bali: Rangda and Barong*, Monographs of the American Ethnological Society, 16, New York, 1949.

_____, *Traditional Balinese Culture*, New York: Columbia University Press, 1970.

_____, *Trance in Bali*, New York: Columbia University Press, 1960.

Coast, John, *Dancers of Bali*, New York: G. P. Putnam, 1953; reissued as *Dancing Out of Bali*, Periplus Editions, 2004.

Covarrubias, Miguel, *Island of Bali*, New York: Knopf, 1937; reprinted Periplus Editions, 2000.

deBoer, Fredrik, "Two Modern Balinese Theater Genres: Sendratari and Drama Gong," in A. Vickers (ed.), *Being Modern in Bali: Image and Change*, New Haven: Yale Southeast Asia Studies Monograph, 43. 1996.

de Zoete, Beryl and Spies, Walter, *Dance and Drama in Bali*, London: Faber and Faber, 1938; reprinted Periplus Editions, 2002.

Dibia, I Wayan, "Arja: A Sung Dance-Drama of Bali: A Study of Change and Transformation," Ph.D dissertation, University of California, Los Angeles, 1992.

_____, *Kecak: The Vocal Chant of Bali*, Denpasar: Hartanto Art Books, 1996.

Eisemann, Fred B. Jr., *Sekala and Niskala, Vol. 1: Essays on Religion and Art*; *Vol. 2: Essays on Society, Tradition and Craft*, Singapore: Periplus Editions, 1990.

Emigh, John, *Masked Performance: The Play of Self and Other in Ritual and Theater*, Philadelphia: University of Pennsylvania, 1996.

Geertz, Hildred, *Images of Power: Balinese Paintings Made for Gregory Bateson and Margeret Mead*, Honolulu: University of Hawaii Press, 1994.

Herbst, Edward, *Voices in Bali: Energies and Perceptions in Vocal Music and Dance Theater*, Hanover and London: Wesleyan University Press, 1997.

Hitchcock, Michael and Norris, Lucy, *Bali, The Imaginary Museum: The Photographs of Walter Spies and Beryl de Zoete*, Kuala Lumpur: Oxford University Press, 1995.

Hobart, Angela, *Dancing Shadows of Bali: Theatre and Myth*, New York: KPI, 1987.

Hobart, Mark, "Live or Dead? How Dialogic is Theatre in Bali?" in Adrian Vickers and I Nyoman Darma Putra (eds.) with Michele Ford, *To Change Bali: Essays in Honour of I Gusti Ngurah Bagus*, Denpasar: Bali Post and the Institute of Social Change and Critical Inquiry, University of Wollongong, 2000.

Hooykaas, C., *Kama and Kala: Materials for the Study of Shadow Theatre in Bali*, Amsterdam: North Holland Publishing, 1973.

_____, *The Lay of Jaya Prana: The Balinese Uriah, Introduction, Texts, Translation and Notes*, London: Luzac, 1958.

Kam, Garrett, *Perceptions of Paradise: Images of Bali in the Arts*, Ubud: Yayasan Dharma Seni Museum Neka, 1993.

_____, *Ramayana in the Arts of Asia*, Singapore: Select Books, 2000.

McPhee, Colin, "The Balinese Wayang Kulit and Its Music," in Jane Belo (ed.), *Traditional Balinese Culture*, New York: Columbia University Press, 1970.

_____, *A Club of Small Men*, 2nd edn, Singapore: Periplus Editions, 2003.

_____, *Music in Bali: A Study in Form and Instrumental Organization in Balinese Orchestral Music*, New Haven: Yale University Press, 1966.

O'Neill, Roma S., "Spirit Possession and Healing Rites in a Balinese Village," MA thesis, University of Melbourne, 1978.

Picard, Michel, *Bali: Cultural Tourism and Touristic Culture*, Singapore: Archipelago Press, 1996.

_____, "Dance and Drama in Bali: The Making of an Indonesian Art Form," in Adrian Vickers (ed.), *Being Modern in Bali: Image and Change*, New Haven: Yale Southeast Asia Studies Monograph, 43, 1996.

Rai S., I Wayan, *Balinese Gamelan Gong Beri*, Denpasar: Prasasti Denpasar, 1998.

Ramseyer, Urs, *The Art and Culture of Bali*, Fribourg: Office du Livre; reprinted Oxford University Press, 1986.

Seebass, Tilman, "Change in Balinese Musical Life: Kebiar in the 1920s and 1930s," in Adrian Vickers (ed.), *Being Modern in Bali: Image and Change*, New Haven: Yale Southeast Asia Studies Monograph, 43, 1996.

Slattum, Judy, *Balinese Masks: Spirits of an Ancient Drama*, 2nd edn, Singapore: Periplus Editions, 2003.

Sugriwa, I G. B. N. Wisnu (ed.), *Bali Arts Festival/Pesta Kesenian Bali*, Denpasar: 1997.

Tenzer, Michael, *Balinese Music*, Singapore: Periplus Editions, 1991.

_____, *Gamelan Gong Kebyar: The Art of Balinese 20th Century Music*, Chicago: University of Chicago Press, 2000.

Vickers, Adrian, *Bali: A Paradise Created*, Ringwood, Victoria: Penguin, 1989.

Zoetmulder, P., *Kalangwan*, The Hague: Martinus Nijhoff, 1974.

Zurbuchen, Mary, *The Language of Balinese Shadow Theater*, Princeton: Princeton University Press, 1987.

Select Discography

Angklung
Bali Record B 234 (cassette), Angklung Santika Budi (Kayu Mas Blod).

Bali Record, B 924 (cassette), Kreasi Angklung, Sekar Jaya.

Balaganjur
Bali Record 1034 (cassette), Kreasi Baru Baleganjur (Banjar Kehen, Keseiman).

King KICC 5197 (World Music Library 97), Balaganjur of Pande and Angklung of Sidan, rec. 1990.

Bamboo Ensembles
Aneka 006 (cassette), Pt. 2: The Best Balinese Traditional Bamboo and Flute Music, Rindik Sanur.

Aneka 289 (cassette), Gong Suling, Abasan, Sangsit.

Aneka 611 (cassette), Jegog Mekepung (Sangkar Agung, Negara)

Bali Record B 124 (cassette), Vol. 1: Joged Bumbung, Semara Yasa, Banjar Bukit Jangkrik, Gianyar.

Bali Record, B 864 (cassette), Suling Tunggal, Gusti Putu Oka, Peliatan, Ubud.

Bali Record, B 879 (cassette), Gamelan Rindik: The Balinese Bamboo and Flute Music, Banjar Tenten, Denpasar.

Buda 92600-02, Musique du Monde: Anthologie des Musiques de Bali, Vol. 1, Traditions Populaires: Formes vocales, musiques de bamboo, rec. 1993.

King KICC 5157 (World Music Library 57), Jegog of Negara, "Suar Agung" dari Desa Sankaragung vs. Sekehe Jegog dari Desa Pendem, rec. 1990.

Dance-Dramas: Arja, Calonarang, Drama Gong, Gambuh, Topeng
Aneka Record 1190 (cassette), Drama Gong: Keris Pengeraksa Jiwa (Sancya Dwipa).

Bali Record 165 (cassette), Topeng Tugek (Carang Sari).

JVC (Victor Entertainment) VICG-60351, Tektekan: The dance-drama "CALON-ARANG" of Krambitan Village.

King KICC 5183 (World Music Library 83), Geguntangan Arja, "Arja Bon Bali," rec. 1990.

Vital Records 501, Music of the Gambuh Theater.

Gamelan Tua and Sacred Ensembles (including Lelambatan)
AMAN 001 Gong Selunding from Tenganan.

AMAN 004 Gambang.

AMAN 005 Gong Gede.
(available from Yayasan Poloisseni and Aman resorts in Indonesia)

Aneka 006 (cassette), Tabuh Lelambatan Klasik, "The Classic Instrumentalia," Gong Gunung Sari, Peliatan, Ubud.

Bali Record, B 956 (cassette), Tabuh Lelambatan Klasik Gong Gede, Petak-Gianyar.

Buda 92602-2, Vol. 3, Anthologie des Musiques de Bali: Musiques Rituelles, rec. 1993.

King KICC 5128 (World Music Library 28), Kecak and Sanghyang of Bali, rec. 1990.

King KICC 5153 (World Music Library 53), Gamelan Gong Gede of Batur, rec. 1990.

King KICC 5182 (World Music Library 82), Gamelan Selonding with Guna Winangumì, Tenganan, rec. 1990.

King KICC 5196 (World Music Library 96), Saron of Singapadu, Bali, rec. 1990.

Maharani (cassette), The Best of Gamelan Slonding 1 and 2: Tenganan, Sanggar Guna Winagun Gamelan Klasik, Tenganan Pegringsingan.

Ocora C559002, Bali: Musique pour le Gong Gde, rec. 1972.

Gender Wayang
Bali Record 643 and 644, Gamelan Gender Vols. 1 & 2 (Kayumas Kaja),1990.

CMP CD 3014, Gender Wayang Pemarwan: Music for the Balinese Sadhow Play "The Mahabharata," rec. 1989.

King KICC 5156 (World Music Library 56), Gender Wayang of Sukawati Village, 1990.

Nonesuch 79718-2 (Explorer Series), Music for the Shadow Play.

Gong Kebyar
AMAN 002 Gong Kebyar from Peliatan [The instruments were made ca. 1931 at the time of the emergence of the Kebyar style] (available from Yayasan Poloisseni and Aman resorts in Indonesia)

Bali Record, B 834 (cassette), Kreasi Pilihan, Khusus Karya, I Nyoman Windha, SSKar.

Bali Record B 1070, Kreasi Gong Kebyar 2001, Vol. 21, Pilihan Terbaik (works of I Nyoman Windha, I Ketut Suardita, I Made Sue, I Wayan Widia).

King KICC 5154 (World Music Library 54), Bali: Gamelan Gong Kebyar of "Eka Cita," Abiankapas Kaja, rec. 1990.

King KICC 5195 (World Music Library 95), Golden Rain/Gong Kebyar of Gunung Sari, rec. 1990.

Long-Distance 122119, Clash of the Gongs, Kebyar from Munduk and Sawan Villages.

Ocora C560057/58, Bali: Les Grands Gong Kebyar des Annees Soixante.

Vital Records 401, Vol. 1, Music of the Gamelan Gong Kebyar, performed by musicians from STSI Denpasar.

Vital Records 402, Vol. 2, Music of the Gamelan Gong Kebyar, Works of I Nyoman Windha, performed by gamelan Mrdangga Giri Kasuma, Candra Metu, and Dharma Kasuma.

Semar Pagulingan, Pelegongan and Semara Dhana
AMAN 003 Gong Semar Pagulingan from Teges Kanginan: Dharma Purwa Jati group (available from Yayasan Poloisseni and Aman resorts in Indonesia)

Aneka 760, Vol. 13 and 761 Vol. 14 (cassettes), Semar Pagulingan Saih Pitu, ASTI.

Bali Record, BRD-02 (cassette) Gamelan Semara Dana, Sekeha Gong Semara Ratih.

Bali Record, BRD 21, 22 and 25 (cassettes), Vols. 2–4, Spirit of Bali: Legong Dance and Gamelan Semara Dana.

Bali Record, B 706 (cassette), Vol. 4, Semar Pagulingan ("Kreasi Baru"), Banjar Teges Peliatan.

CMP Records CD 3008, Gamelan Semar Pegulingan Saih Pitu (Kamasan), 1991.

ÇUDAMANI: The Seven-Tone Gamelan Orchestra from the Village of Pengosekan, Bali (Vital Records 440). [The virtuosic musicians of Çudamani, led by Dewa Putu Berata, play on an unusual type of hybrid gamelan orchestra created in the 1980s.]

King KICC 5180 (World Music Library 80), Gamelan Semar Pagulingan of Gunung Jati.

Lyrichord 7408, Music of Bali: The Gamelan Semar Pagulingan of Ketewel, rec. 1996.

Nonesuch 79720, Bali: Gamelan Semar Pagulingan, The Gamelan of the Love God directed by Made Lebah. [Music from Teges Kanginan played on the gamelan formerly kept by Colin McPhee in his house in Sayan.]

Odyssey Music Distributors, OMD J8165-I, TJ-1060 (cassette), "Sweet and Intoxicating Gamelan," "Mandala Jati," Semar Peguling-an Ensemble of Teges Village, Peliatan, Bali.

World Music Library, KICW-1068, Gamelan Semar Pagulingan of Binoh Village.

Anthologies

Auvidis/Ethnic B 6769, Bali, Musique Du Nord-Ouest: Joged, Balaganjur, Gong Druwe, Angklung.

Buda 92601-02, Musique du Monde, Vol. 2, Anthologie des Musiques de Bali, Gamelan Virtuoses: Gamelan Gong, Gong Suling, Gamelan Angklung.

Buda 92603-02, Musique du Monde, Vol. 4, Anthologie des Musiques de Bali, Traditions Savantes: Gambuh, Arja, Wayang Ramayana, Wayang Parwa, Semar Pagulingan Saih Pitu, Pelegongan, Joged Pingitan.

Jukung Music, JKN-001, "The Works of I Wayan Gandra", Genta Bhuana Sari, Peliatan.

King KICC 5126 (World Music Library, 26), The Gamelan Music of Bali: Gong Kebyar, Semar Pagulingan, Gong Gede, Gender Wayang, Selunding, Balaganjur.

King KICC 5127 (World Music Library, 27), Music in Bali: Cakepung, Gambang, Genggong, Gong Luang, kidung, Arja Geguntangan, Joged Bumbung, Jegog, rec. 1990.

Nonesuch 9 79204-2, Bali: Gamelan and Kecak: Gong Kebyar, Gender Wayang, Kecak, Selunding, Gong Suling, Genggong, Balaganjur, Baris, rec. 1987.

Nonesuch 9 79196-2, Music from the Morning of the World: Kecak, Gong Kebyar, Gender Wayang, Angklung, Gambuh, Genggong, Pelegongan, rec. 1966.

Nonesuch 79716-2 (Explorer Series), Golden Rain.

Rykodisc, RCD 10315, Music for the Gods: The Fahnestock South Sea Expedition (Library of Congress Endangered Music Project), Indonesia: Semar Pagulingan, Gender Wayang, Kecak, Digitalized remastered transfers from the 1941 Expedition made by Bruce and Sheridan Fahnestock.

World Arbiter CD 2001 The Roots of Gamelan Bali, 1928 (ref. www.arbiterrecords.com).

Miscellaneous

Bali Record, BRD-07 (cassette), Kecak Dance Live, Fire Dance, Bone, Gianyar.

Bali Record, B 935 (cassette), Kreasi Genjek Stress, Jasri-Karangasem.

Bridge Records BCD9019, Kecak from Bali: A Balinese Music Drama.

New Music

Akira, Geinoh Yamashirogumi, compositions and conducting by Yamashiro Shoji, JVC JMI1001. Japan. [Large chorus and instrumental samples, including gamelan; soundtrack for the animated sci-fi film "Akira."]

Balinese Music in America: Gamelan Sekar Jaya, directed by Wayne Vitale (Gong Kebyar) and Carla Fabrizio (Angklung). GSJ-011. Compositions by I Wayan Beratha, I Nyoman Windha, I Ketut Partha, Dewa Putu Berata and Wayne Vitale.

Endless Wonderer, JMCD-004. Collaboration of GOMA da Didgeridoo (Japan) and Gong Padang Tegal, Ubud.

Evan Ziporyn/Gamelan Galak Tika: Amok!, Tire Fire, New World Records. [Evan Ziporyn is one of the few composers to integrate entire ensembles of Western instruments with the gamelan instead of single instruments, as in his metrically vigorous "Tire Fire" for Balinese gamelan and electric guitars and keyboards.]

Evan Ziporyn/Cantaloupe Music (2001), THIS IS NOT A CLARINET (includes solo clarinet versions of two Balinese melodies, "Pengrangrang Gde" and "Bindu Semara" (as taught on Gender Wayang by I Wayan Suweca and I Made Konolan).

Evan Ziporyn/Cantaloupe Music (2002), SHADOW BANG (collaboration with dalang I Wayan Wija plus clarinet, cello, guitar, bass, keyboard and percussion.

Evan Ziporyn/Cantaloupe Music (2004), SO MUCH PERCUSSION, "Melody Competition", percussion sextet based on West Balinese gamelan Jegog Mebarung.

Evan Ziporyn/New Albion (2004), KAMAR MUSIC, includes "Ngaben" (tribute to the Bali bomb victims) for gamelan and orchestra; also "Pondok," four movements for piano based on Balinese musical forms.

Jogcak, AMAN 333. [Marrying the two ensembles of Cak and the Jegog results in this unusual blend of vocal and bamboo music where the chorus rides on the bamboo tubes.] (available from Yayasan Poloisseni and Aman resorts in Indonesia).

New World Records, CD 80430-2, American Works for Balinese Gamelan produced by Evan Ziporyn, Michael Tenzer, Wayne Vitale, performed by Gamelan Sekar Jaya, Seka Gong Abdi Budaya, and students at STSI Denpasar.

SUN VICL-61316, Collaboration of UA (Japan) and Çudamani (Bali).

World Language Rhythm vBr 2117 2, Ketu, directed by Reinhard Flatischler. [Includes collaborations with Jegog group Suar Agung as well as Zakir Hussain (India), Leonard Ito (Japan), Hiedrun Hoffman (Germany), Wolfgang Pusching and Flatischler (Austria).]

VCDs

Note: Video cassette discs (not to be confused with DVDs) are widely available on Bali. Word has it that they will play in most DVD players. These are not compatible with all systems world-wide and may will not play in your computers. VCDs have been made of nearly every popular form and are available in cassette shops throughout Bali.

Acknowledgments

The authors would like to acknowledge the skills that they have gained from their many teachers. There are so many great Balinese artists that we have studied with that it is impossible to mention them all.

I Wayan Dibia would like to thank his late parents, I Wayan Geriya and Ni Nyoman Rindi (both renowned dancers and his first teachers), the late I Made Kredek (Baris), the late Pande Kenyir (Jauk), the late I Nyoman Kakul (Topeng), the late I Nyoman Kembur (Barong), I Gede Geruh (Gambuh), I Made Jimat (Jauk), I Wayan Beratha (gamelan), I Gusti Bagus Nyoman Panji (former director of the High School of Performing Arts or KOKAR/SMKI), Prof. Dr I Wayan Mertha Sutedja and Prof. Dr I Made Bandem (former directors of ASTI/ISI Denpasar).

Rucina Ballinger began her studies of Balinese dance with I Nyoman Wenten in California and continued with the late I Nyoman Kakul (Baris, Gambuh, Topeng), Sang Ayu Ketut Muklin (Legong Keraton), Ni Ketut Arini Alit (Taruna Jaya, Legong Keraton, and other Kebyar dances) and I Ketut Kantor and I Ketut Wirtawan (Topeng). She studied with many great musicians and dancers while an active member of Gamelan Sekar Jaya in California from 1979 to 1985, including her co-author, I Wayan Dibia. To all of the performers in Bali, she extends her warm gratitude. In particular, Arini Alit provided information on Kebyar and Legong, as well as hours of discussion (not to mention laughter). I K. Kantor, I K. Wirtawan, I N. Cerita, I K. Kodi, I. B. Wirjana, I W. Narta and Ni G. A. Raka Rasmin all gave generously of their time. And last, but not least, Agung, Anom and Arie put up with my obsession for many months—my heartfelt thanks to my "club of men."

Barbara Anello wishes to acknowledge and thank Ida Pedanda Gede Wayan Datah of Geria Krotok, Budakeling, for his instruction; Ida Wayan Padang and Ida Made Basma of Geria Tubuh, Abang, Karangasem, for the dance; Ida Wayan Taman for his story; Kakiang Belawa and Aji Poleng, gone but remembered; Ida Bagus Dibia, remembered; Anak Agung Raka Bawa, for the first midnight shadow puppet performances; and Alicia Martin and Peter and Barbara Tollitt for adventures shared and kindness shown.

Wayne Vitale gave valuable insight into gamelan music. M. Tenzer, K. Worthy, W. Vitale, J. Diamond, K. Devereaux, P. Yampolsky, E. Herbst, A. Jeanson, A. Timar, K. Tetsuro, D. Myers and R. Brown helped with the compilation of the discography. Barbara Anello read through and edited the manuscript. Garrett Kam, a performer and writer himself, went over the manuscript numerous times, giving generously of his time and knowledge. Our heartfelt gratitude goes to him.

The illustrations are by Barbara Anello and the photographs are from the collections of the authors and illustrator, unless otherwise stated. Any omissions or errors are the fault of the authors and we apologize in advance for these. Our intention is to introduce the beauty of Balinese performing arts to a wider audience.

Mesolah satmaka ngayah ring Sanghyang Widhi Wasa
Dancing is like praying to God

Picture Credits

top (t); bottom (b); center (c); left (l); right (r)

Barbara Anello, front endpaper—hc edit. (l, r) [Legong Untung Surapati reproduced courtesy of Sheraton Laguna Nusa Dua], pp. 2–3, 7 (all) [reproduced courtesy of Mary Bradley and Pauline Loong], 10 (t, b), 15 (all), 17 (tr), 18 (l), 20 (c), 22 (tl), 23 (t, b), 25 (b), 26–7 (b), 29, 31, 34 (t), 35 (b), 40 (c), 41 (b), 43, 45, 46 (b), 48–9 (all), 52 [reproduced courtesy of Alicia Martin], 52–3 (c), 56 (t), 57 (all), 58 (t), 59, 60 (t), 63 (all) [Hanuman reproduced courtesy of Peter and Venta Richter; Jatayu re-produced courtesy of Hans Meinke], 68 (t) [reproduced courtesy of The Ascott, Jakarta], 70 (t), 77 (b), 78–9 (all) [Legong Untung Suripati reproduced courtesy of Peter and Venta Richter], 80 (all) [small images reproduced courtesy of Peter and Barbara Tollitt; large image reproduced courtesy of LeMeridian Nirwana Golf & Spa Resort, Tanah Lot], 82 (tl), 83 (r), 84 (t), 86 (t), 87, 90 (t, b), 92 (bl), 96 (t), 97 (t), 102 (t)
ARTI Foundation, p. 101 (t)
I Gusti Made Aryantha, pp. 13 (b), 18–19 (b), 21 (c), 22 (bl, c), 24 (all), 27 (tr), 30 (b), 32 (tl), 32–33 (b), 36 (b), 55, 77 (t), 81 (b), 84 (b), 88 (t), 89 (b), 95 (all), 97 (b), 99 (b)
Rucina Ballinger, pp. 9 (t), 14 (t), 16 (t) [collection of], 33 (t), 35 (t), 37 (t, b), 39 (b), 41 (t), 44, 64–5 (c), 66, 67 (br, r), 76 (b), 88 (b), 89 (t), 91 (t), 94 (t), 100 (t), 102 (b)
Iwan Darmawan, pp. 16 (b), 21 (r), 38 (b), 74 (b), 86 (b), 96 (b), 99 (rc)
I Wayan Dibia, pp. 12 (t), 69 [collection of], 81 [collection of], 92 (t), 98 (t, b), 99 (t), 103 (t) [collection of]
Gamelan Sekar Jaya, p. 103
Rio Helmi, p. 93 (b)
Garrett Kam, pp. 75 (b), 82 (t), 83 (b)
I Made Lila, p. 14 (bc)
Gill Marais, pp. 6, 11, 12 (b), 13 (t), 14 (br), 17 (tl), 28 (b), 30 (t), 38 (t), 40 (t), 55, 58 (b), 61, 75 (t), 81 (t), 91 (b), 92–3 (b)
Eric Oey, pp. 8 (t), 25 (t), 56 (b), 60 (b), 76 (b)
Peter Sloane, pp. 21 (l), 93 (t)
I Nyoman Sumaartha, p. 100 (b)
I Gusti Raka Panji Tisna, pp. 28 (t), 34 (b), 46 (t), 82 (b)
Walter Spies Foundation, pp. 14 (bl), 53 (t) [reproduced courtesy of Hedi Hinzler and the Walter Spies Foundation of Holland]
Warini, 94 [collection of]
Rachel Williams, p. 39 (t)
Matt Wyatt, pp. 4, 8 (b), 9 (b), 19 (t), 20 (t), 40 (bl), 42, 47 (t, b), 50, 51, 53 (b), 54, 62 (t, b), 64 (l), 65 (t, b), 67 (tl, tr, bl), 68 (b), 71, 72–3 (all), 74 (t), 101 (b)
Scott Zielinski, pp. 70 (b), 85